Advance Praise for Myles Weber's Work

"Myles Weber brings to his essays and reviews on the subject of modern theatre a depth of insight, inquisitiveness, and humor that I can only call extraordinary. A successful playwright in his own right, his criticism enjoys a remarkable convergence of practical as well as scholarly experience of the genre. What he has to say is uniquely valuable, intelligent and fiercely principled."

—John Witte, Editor, *Northwest Review*

"In these beautifully written and provocative pieces, Myles Weber introduces us to and writes knowledgeably about a wide range of American and English plays and playwrights. It is not necessary to agree with everything he says to find his essays full of incisive commentary and witty observations."

—Jackson R. Bryer, Co-editor, *The Selected Letters of Eugene O'Neill*

"Weber's intelligence and integrity are unsurpassed by anyone writing about the American theatre today. To find his equal, one must go back half a century, to Mary McCarthy in her youthful prime, when she was both Broadway's scourge and its conscience."

—John W. Crowley, Chair and Professor of English, The University of Alabama at Tuscaloosa

"In *Middlebrow Annoyances*, Weber molds a half-dozen years of his essays and reviews into a state-of-the-art statement both sobering and hopeful. An outsider with insider knowledge and understanding, he is unafraid of controversy and complaint, is willing to take to task even such contemporary icons as Arthur Miller, Edward Albee, August Wilson, and David Mamet. In fact, Myles Weber is at his best and most engaging when offering overview assessments of the biggest names in American theatre over the past fifty years.

Middlebrow Annoyances is an agitating pleasure to read; it will enlighten the newcomers in the audience and challenge the veterans—and the nation's theater will be the better for both of these results."

—Stephen Corey, Associate Editor, *The Georgia Review*

MIDDLEBROW ANNOYANCES

AMERICAN DRAMA IN THE 21ST CENTURY

MYLES WEBER

Gival Press

Arlington, Virginia

MIDDLEBROW ANNOYANCES: AMERICAN DRAMA IN THE 21ST CENTURY.
Copyright © 2003 by Myles Weber.

All rights reserved under International and Pan-American Copyright Conventions.
Printed in the United States of America.

With the exception of brief quotations in the body of critical articles or reviews, no part of the book may be reproduced or transmitted in any form or by any means, graphic, electronic, or mechanical, including photocopying, recording, taping, or by any information storage or retrieval system, without the permission in writing from the publisher.

Published by Gival Press, an imprint of Gival Press, LLC.
For information please write:
Gival Press, LLC, P. O. Box 3812,
Arlington, Virginia 22203.
Website: givalpress.com

First Edition

ISBN 1-928589-20-0
Library of Congress Card Number 200218636
Photo of Myles Weber by Jeff LiaBraaten.
Format and design by Ken Schellenberg.

"Tennessee Williams on the Incline" was first published in slightly different form (under the title "Catching the Streetcar") in *The Sewanee Review*, vol. 110, no. 3, Summer 2002. Copyright 2002 by the University of the South. Reprinted with permission of the editor.

Other parts of this collection originally appeared in slightly different form in the following publications:
New England Review: "Buzz" (under the title "Two Times Two: Some Notes on Our Contemporary Theater" in vol. 23, no. 2, Spring 2002), "Tony Kushner Talking" (in vol. 21, no. 3, Summer 2000), "David Hare On Broadway" (under the title "David Hare's *Via Dolorosa*" in vol. 22, no. 1, Winter 2001), "Where Arthur Miller Stands" (in vol. 22, no. 4, Fall 2001), and "David Mamet in Theory and Practice" (in vol. 21, no. 2, Spring 2000).

The Kenyon Review: "Seeking a Post-Ibsenian Playwright" (in vol. 23, no. 1, Winter 2001) and "The Goldilocks Formula" (in vol. 25, no. 2, Spring 2003).

The Chattahoochee Review: "Direct Solicitation to Agent" (in vol. 19, no. 1, Fall 1998), "Middlebrow Annoyances" (in vol. 21, no. 2, Winter 2001), and "Hot New Plays!" (in vol. 20, no. 2, Winter 2000).

The Georgia Review: "Oppositional Playwrights/Conformist Views" (in vol. 54, no. 1, Spring 2000) and part of "A British Mini-Boom" (in vol. 56, no. 3, Fall 2002)

Northwest Review: "Light Hitters" (in vol. 40, no. 1, 2002), "Scary Balding White Men in Suits" (in vol. 40, no. 3, 2002), and "Holding History" (in vol. 39, no. 3, 2001).

Partisan Review: "Edward Albee: The Contrarian Messiah" (under the title "The Life of a Playwright" in vol. 68, no. 2, Spring 2001).

Southern Humanities Review: "Neil Simon on Autopilot" (in vol. 36, no. 1, Winter 2002).

Harrington Gay Men's Fiction Quarterly: "Moonlighting in Hollywood" (in vol. 4, no. 2, Fall 2002).

For my parents.

Contents

Introduction: Seeking a Post-Ibsenian Playwright	9
Buzz	14
Oppositional Playwrights, Conformist Views	21
Tony Kushner Talking	24
Direct Solicitation to Agent	29
Hot New Plays!	34
David Hare on Broadway	41
A British Mini-Boom	44
Tom Stoppard, American	49
Political Stages	52
Light Hitters	58
Scary Balding White Men in Suits: Anna Deavere Smith Talks to Us	66
Where Arthur Miller Stands	69
Holding History	75
Edward Albee: The Contrarian Messiah	82
August Wilson Grounded	86
Middlebrow Annoyances	92
Neil Simon on Autopilot	99
Moonlighting in Hollywood	102
Tennessee Williams on the Incline	110
David Mamet in Theory and Practice	116
The Goldilocks Formula	122
Wither [sic] Theater?	128
Afterword: A Not So Safe Space	133

Introduction: Seeking a Post-Ibsenian Playwright

"When you deal with Ibsen, you deal with what the middle class considered indecent, disgusting, amateurish, poisonous," explains Stella Adler in a posthumous collection of lectures, *Stella Adler on Ibsen, Strindberg, and Chekhov* (Knopf, 1999). "The criticism of him was furious in the middle-class newspapers." Unlike subsequent chapters, which move scene-by-scene through the major plays of Strindberg and Chekhov, Adler's expansive analysis of Ibsen focuses more generally on his critique of institutions and their grip on the individual. She goes on at such great length, in fact, that this matter overshadows the rest of the book and taints her analysis of Ibsen's successor playwrights, which I believe is her main point: that modern drama, which began with Ibsen, is a perpetual rephrasing of his assault on middle-class convention.

According to Adler, Ibsen neatly divides society into three types: the Idealist who accepts society's illusions, including the most treacly misrepresentations of marriage (this, Adler claims, is the category into which the vast majority fall); the Compromiser who "knows the truth but settles for something else"; and the least common type, the Realist who "knows the truth but wants and tries to change it," often paying the ultimate price, even at her own hand à la Hedda Gabler.

I should probably admit right here that I consider this sort of analysis self-glorifying drivel, though it may accurately describe Ibsen's schematics. I object because it justifies the contempt many playwrights, directors, and actors show their audience and the public at large, whom they consider dolts (that is, Idealists). As I see it, the vast majority of people are Compromisers who want and try to change things but not at the expense of what still proves useful in the status quo. Like Realists, Compromisers understand the God does not exist, but they continue to live as if He does. They have children to raise and morality seems to help. Is that foolish or heroic?

Of Ibsen's hero, the Realist who bravely unmasks harmful illusions, Adler says, "He sees the evil, denounces it." Her example of a "radical realist" is Byron, who risked being ostracized by having a sexual affair with his sister. I can think of other radical realists: Buddha, Jesus Christ, the Marquis de Sade, Charles Manson, Jeffrey Dahmer. Each of these men refused to let himself be compromised by middle-class convention or its historical equivalent. The point is clear: the moment we place limits on the individual's assault on convention, we have compromised. We are, nearly all of us, Compromisers.

At the end of *A Doll's House*, Nora – for too long an Idealist who accepted marriage for what it was not – becomes a Realist. The scales fall from her eyes: she leaves the infantilizing, disloyal husband she does not love, but she also abandons her children without a second thought. That abandonment is the only thing about the play that remains shocking to this day, and it stems from what Ibsen and Adler laud as Nora's refusal to compromise. A form of Phariseeism is at work here: those in the theater who publicly berate society for its ills, no matter how recklessly, credit themselves for the changes that ensue when yeoman's work is done at ground level by a silent army of Compromisers.

I propose we cultivate a new American playwright, a post-Ibsenian writer whose plays feature characters who from the opening scene have already pondered their bourgeois condition – who, like us, have seen *A Doll's House* and remember how it ends. If Adler's claim is accurate – if all modern drama exists in Ibsen's shadow – we need to step out from the dark form he casts. Adler reports that Ibsen gave us for the first time characters who, unlike Iago, were not clearly designated good or bad, but were in flux between the two. But what Ibsen did not give us were characters who recognize the subtleties of argument the way an audience member does. The mayor speaks on behalf of the state, while his brother, a doctor, speaks on behalf of the people, though ironically the people view him as their enemy. Nora's actions say, "Defy convention, no matter the cost to others"; Torvald's say, "Respect convention, no matter the cost to yourself." Nothing can be worked through, no shading is permitted. Carrying this forward from one generation of playwrights to the next, you get Arthur Miller. "Miller's play *The Price* is Ibsenian," Adler states, "one brother says you shouldn't have cared for Father, you should have been a doctor. The other says, I have the responsibility to care for Father. There is a fight on stage – who is right? This is Ibsen's contribution to theater. No modern problems are really solvable. Ibsen makes you understand that the overall thinking in a modern play is muddled. There are really no ground rules."

But there *are* ground rules: keep the argument rigidly two-sided. Disallow compromise. Don't create characters who have synthesized conflicting points of view prior to the action.

Clearly, not all contemporary playwrights are as baldly Ibsenian as Miller, but I accept Adler's claim: "All modern plays have Ibsenian needs." Modern theater is the theater of engagement, of social criticism, and its works can generally be categorized under realism – a category Adler insists is almost impossible to escape. In part, her argument is this: contemporary dramatists construct a critique of middle-class convention in their plays; Ibsen constructed a critique of middle-class convention in his plays, and he was a modern realist; therefore, contemporary dramatists are modern realists. It's not sound logic, but she has a point. Nearly all modern playwrights attempt the same thing, regardless of style or method. They are colleagues in what Robert Brustein termed "the theatre of revolt." Consider Edward Albee's oeuvre: he has employed a succession of writing styles, including realism, as the material has demanded, but in each play he makes the same critique of the bourgeois mind – of its stupidity and dullness and its capacity for evil. And writers who have managed to avoid realism – Christopher Durang, Nicky Silver, and a number of feminists authors – make a similar critique, always of an identical, grotesque middle-class family.

It should come as no surprise that Adler was right about this: she was a singular force in American theater for over half a century. She shaped generations of directors, playwrights, and actors at her Actors Studio – later Conservatory – in New York City. "After Ibsen," she prophesied, "all writers are going to deal with the social moment." And having instructed American writers for fifty years that they must deal with the social moment, her prophecy is now self-fulfilled. But her imperative is precisely what we must move beyond, improve upon, or transcend – even in realism.

Clearly, mine is not the first call for a new modern playwright. But previous calls have gone unheeded. The temptation is too great: theater provides the perfect opportunity for writers to puff themselves up. Contemporary drama continues to be written by artists who believe that the vast majority of the audience fits Ibsen's category of Idealist and needs to be educated. ("They just want to be 'happy,'" Adler insists. "They want the illusion.") Only theater folk manage to remove their blinders, or so theater folk believe. The rest of us remain deserving of their contempt.

Of course, there are practical reasons why Ibsenian drama persists: it's easy. With implausibly rigid points of view in place, conflict can be generated between characters at will. And there are legitimate fears about where a post-Ibsenian drama might lead: to a Quentin Tarantino movie or *Seinfeld*, the show about nothing in which characters manage only to smirk at each other, or fight over a bagel. But I'm convinced that the promise of what we might achieve is worth the risk. If we fail, we're stuck with the equivalent of a nihilistic Hollywood movie or a smug sit-com, but if we succeed, we're treated to electrifying characters who resonate with the people who attend our plays. If we do nothing, we get what we deserve: father and son arguing Position A and Position B, respectively; a preachy, flat-footed encounter between a clever homeless man and a moronic business executive; happy parents eating their children, or vice versa. And not a compelling character in sight. Granted, in works by Miller or Albee, the result can be powerful. But in the hands of their less skilled progeny, it's not powerful, and it's not very entertaining.

So much of modern playwriting seems motivated by revenge: against the playwright's parents for being imperfect, against men, against Hollywood, against God for not existing. Revenge fits the Ibsenian mold quite nicely, which may help explain the longevity of the type. August Strindberg also seems motivated by revenge, but as a psychological dramatist, and an anti-feminist, he shatters the mold. As Adler explains, "In Ibsen, people are trapped by society. In Strindberg they are trapped by themselves."

Could Strindberg's example release us from the grip of Ibsen? "Strindberg believed that the modern world doesn't care what happens but how it happens," Adler writes. "He wants to know the machinery behind it." This suggests a possible shift in focus that would allow characters to absorb and negotiate more than one point of view. But although Eugene O'Neill and other modern playwrights greatly admired him, Strindberg seems too much an entity unto himself to serve as a point of embarkation for a new line of drama. As Albert Camus once said of Truman Capote, he is "a genius, *sui generis*" – and that's not a compliment. Strindberg is fascinating, but he is not a vehicle *to* anywhere. If anything, he is a trap. "Once you start dealing with a Strindberg theme," Adler explains, "you are dragged into the deepest abyss, from which you cannot emerge."

The third major dramatist about whom Adler lectures – Chekhov – may be of greater use, though he also leads us ultimately back to the Ibsen conundrum. If there is a pervasive theme to Chekhov's plays, Adler states, it's that materialism has the power to kill the soul – or, more vaguely, that we are witnessing "the destruction of beauty in the world." This is what lends an air of sadness to all of Chekhov's works. But what is the ultimate cause of that destruction? The vulgarization of culture brought about by a burgeoning middle class – you see where this is heading. Still, there is much we can take away from Chekhov. "*Uncle Vanya* makes no point," Adler declares. "Chekhov said a play need not make a point." Sell that idea to NBC, and you've got a hit comedy. But there is a significant difference between a Chekhov play and a *Seinfeld* script, and it pertains to audience. Chekhov's audience "recognized Shakespeare," Adler reports. Members of the contemporary American audience are credited with recognizing television personalities. That difference in perceived sophistication gave Chekhov the luxury of writing about inward lives, at the expense of plot.

The new playwright I champion could learn a great deal from *Uncle Vanya* and Chekhov's other pointless plays. Lacking Chekhov's genius, my new playwright might have to reinject plot into the equation, which I favor; more important, the new playwright should assume a savvy, intelligent audience like Chekhov had. I don't celebrate contemporary theater's great weakness – its lack of popularity – but if that is the reality, playwrights ought to exploit it. Writers for the stage have no mass audience to pander to. They should admit who's sitting in those uncomfortable seats: a small but sharp-minded group of people who have forsaken the nonentertainment of television. This is an audience that has no need for a straw argument designed to Make Them Think. They can think for themselves – that's what got them to the theater in the first place. The playwright's job is to entertain with his art. I repeat for shock value: the playwright's job is to entertain with his art. When successfully executed, for an intelligent audience, a work of drama carries thematic weight and social relevance automatically. It cannot be avoided – I've tried.

The actor's craft that Adler learned from Stanislavsky, and which she says is necessary to perform Ibsen, Strindberg, and especially Chekhov, need not be abandoned or altered. What needs to change are the characters themselves. "Strindberg is the first Freudian playwright," Adler tells us. "The complexity of the inner man carries his plays." What we need now, in addition to playwrights familiar with Freud, are characters familiar with Freud, to keep pace with audience members familiar with Freud. And with Marx, Darwin, Einstein, as well as television personalities. Insulating Idealist characters in an implausible bubble of naïveté so the playwright can mock or educate them is a flimsy technique that must be abandoned.

The gross condescension of actors and playwrights to the middle class and those who aspire to it is appalling. Explaining her approach to the character Natasha,

Andrei's social-climbing wife in *Three Sisters*, Adler gloats, "When the working class gets a car, it wants two cars. It just wants more money and more comfort. You must accept their vulgarity because they don't want to change." I am a thirty-eight-year-old American with two advanced degrees. My parents graduated from high school. My maternal grandmother, God rest her soul, spoke in this manner: "We was pert' near home when your uncle Ned begun ta holler." In the course of three generations, my family has moved securely into the middle class, yet I've never owned a car or a home and I see nothing contemptible about my comforts: a bed, a couch, a desk. I may be an anachronism, but what the theater community has to understand is that the entire theater-going public is an anachronism. And it is growing smaller and more anachronistic each day.

"From Ibsen on, especially in Strindberg, you see that the mixture of the classes destroys," Adler tells her students. "If an aristocratic woman sleeps with a coachman for some reason, she kills herself. She has to. It's a lousy mix." *Miss Julie*, *A Doll's House*, *Uncle Vanya*, and the other great plays of modern European drama are indispensable works, but their direct application to American culture has its limitations. We've never had a mature class system. We have extreme income disparity, we have racial and ethnic division, but we do not have a well-delineated structure of social class. Thus, our classes do not mix tragically. They just mix. And the vulgarization of culture is no threat to us either – our culture has always been vulgar. What the theater community must recognize is that their audience comprises persons like themselves: children or grandchildren of the working class who, thanks to the sustained growth of the American economy, now have the option of pursuing money, comfort, a car, two cars – but who have chosen in a small way, for one evening, to forsake their most vulgar pursuits and attend live theater. Our playwrights, directors, and actors must stop condescending to the audience. The audience members are not ditsy Noras, oblivious to institutional hypocrisy. Nor are the playwrights heroic Noras slamming the door as they leave. If anything, we are, all of us, Torvalds just after Nora's departure – privileged beyond most people's dreams, but stunned by our loss and trying to make sense of the world.

[2001]

Buzz

"Our American theater sucks," declared Michael Cunningham in an interview with Tony Kushner at the height of *Angels in America*'s popularity. Kushner agreed there probably was, in percentage terms, more bad drama produced in our culture than bad prose fiction, bad poetry, or even bad film. Playwright Suzan-Lori Parks makes the same point in her essay "Elements of Style": in no other genre these days, she laments, is the writing so awful.

Why should this be? Kushner offered the plausible explanation that money lures the talented away to other fields; only the chronically unemployable continue to plug away in theater. But Parks faults the slim intentions of the artists: the entire institutional apparatus of theater encourages works intended not to delight, fascinate, or awe the audience but rather to elicit a safe political reaction – "to discuss some issue," as Parks puts it. The buzz from a topical play can catapult the work, the playwright, the production, even the theater company out of obscurity. There is every professional reason, then, to write bad drama of this particular issue-oriented sort.

Rebecca Gilman, a successful Chicago playwright, is riding a national wave of buzz generated by two recent works – *Spinning into Butter* and *Boy Gets Girl* (both published by Faber and Faber in 2000) – that each discuss an issue: liberal racism in the first case, violence against women in the second. By way of contrast, Kenneth Lonergan took a different route from obscurity, and I believe it spared him the necessity of writing bad plays. Lonergan worked with various theater companies in New York – Second Stage, the New Group, Naked Angels – but finally rose to prominence by following the money trail to film. His screenplay credits include the Hollywood comedy *Analyze This* and the independent feature *You Can Count on Me*, which he also directed, and which deservedly won him wider praise than any single stage production could.

Like Gilman, Lonergan has two plays currently published in trade paperback editions. Both works display the acumen and modesty of a truly gifted artist. *The Waverly Gallery* (Grove, 2000) chronicles the final undignified months in the life of Gladys Green, who – hard of hearing and losing her memory – just likes to yammer. "Everyone needs someone to talk to," she explains, "otherwise you'd just go nutty. I love to talk to people." A one-time lawyer, but now the naïve proprietress of a money-losing art gallery in Greenwich Village, Gladys is provided the gratuitous résumé of a political radical who found herself in Germany just as the Nazis were consolidating power. But there is an aura of the playwright's autobiography clinging to Gladys and her family that may account for stock elements of her personal history.

A basically endearing woman, Gladys alarms those with responsibility for her well-being when she invites an unknown artist to sleep in the backroom of her gallery. She compounds that error, in the eyes of her daughter Ellen and grandson Daniel, by imposing her hospitable inclinations on them and, for good measure, misplacing Ellen's Vermont cabin in a neighboring state.

ELLEN: She's getting worse.
DANIEL: Oh, she's definitely getting worse, Mom.

A play about a character with a frustratingly disordered mind, who is in a frustrating and combative relationship with her family, could have been itself a frustrating experience. But *The Waverly Gallery* is instead an unusually pleasurable juggling act of overlapping, misdirected dialogue. The grandson, Daniel, addresses the audience at regular intervals. That works to good effect, in part because we need some order imposed on the narrative, but also because the author's language is precise and deft. This is the case in his stage directions and character descriptions as well. Don, the possibly talentless artist, is described as "a careful, hardworking and detail-fixated person who devotes a lot of his mental energy to very slowly and carefully arriving at the wrong conclusion." As much an author surrogate as grandson Daniel, Don feels compelled to reproduce on canvas the image of a macramé decoration his mother once made, to preserve for posterity the domestic details of his family history.

With its gestures toward autobiography, its painfully humorous representations of dementia, and Daniel's apt if obvious conclusion – "it must be worth a lot to be alive" – *The Waverly Gallery* reminded me of Christopher Durang's *The Marriage of Bette and Boo*, as well as Thornton Wilder's *Our Town*, a stark, horrific play dismissed as soft by those with faulty memories. Like those works, *The Waverly Gallery* confronts honestly the unpleasant aspects of its subject matter. Gladys, with her fumbled insulin injections and incessant word salad, ends up completely alienating her grandson, who lives in the same building and who wishes to preserve memories of an unfaded, robust Gladys. "She rang my doorbell so much I stopped answering it all the time," Daniel confesses. "Instead I'd just go to the door and look through the peephole to make sure she was OK, and then I'd watch this weird little convex image of her turn around in the hallway and go back into her apartment." For her part, Daniel's mother, Ellen, wishes her own 85-year-old mother peacefully dead. "[B]ut Dr. Wagner says there's nothing wrong with her physically," she tells Daniel. "She could go on like this for another ten years."

It is the strongest praise I can give the playwright that these acts of disloyalty, hurtful and selfish as they are, can be read as tragic signs of both hopelessness and, ultimately, love.

Like *The Waverly Gallery*, Lonergan's previous play, *This Is Our Youth* (Overlook, 2000), features characters trying to evoke a less corrupted, more energetic past. But, age nineteen to twenty-one, they are only yet embarking on the young adulthood they are trying to reclaim. Their current misadventures are self-conscious attempts to manufacture fond memories before they mature into the roles currently held by their impeccably responsible, upper-middle-class parents.

The characters themselves are completely aware of their impending metamorphoses. Warren, the younger of two male characters, is told by his mentor and abusive friend Dennis, "I'm like a one-man youth culture for you pathetic assholes. You're gonna remember your youth as like a gray stoned haze punctuated by a series of beatings from your fuckin' Dad, and like, *my* jokes. God *damn!*" Jessica, whom Warren has designs on, offers an equally clear appraisal: "[R]ight now you're all like this rich little pot-smoking burnout rebel, but ten years from now you're gonna be like a plastic *surgeon* reminiscing about how wild you used to be."

The story is this: Warren has stolen $15,000 from his estranged father who, though not a criminal himself, is in business with criminals. Dennis hatches a plot to use the stolen money to finance a quick drug-selling scheme, return the stolen cash before the theft is detected, and walk away with a neat profit. (Even as they stall at becoming their parents, it is clear that they *are* their parents.) Lonergan includes a few half-hearted nods to nihilism:

DENNIS: What is gonna happen to you, man?
WARREN: What is gonna happen to anybody? Who cares?

But the more prominent authorial tone is caution: characters play with fire, hoping not to get burned. Still, some do. Dennis's dealer friend, Stuey, dies of a drug overdose, and we are told that Warren's older sister was murdered years before at about this same age, as she passed through her own rebellious stage.

Set in 1982, *This Is Our Youth* owes a lot to *Less Than Zero*, Bret Easton Ellis's novel from that era. Both feature a set of young, privileged characters whose self-inflicted injuries are only as severe as they themselves permit. Family wealth acts as a safety net but, alas, some characters choose to stretch the weave too far and slip through.

Lonergan's play also pays homage to *American Buffalo*, David Mamet's own three-character drama involving petty theft, the pawning of useless goods, and other vague dealings in a half-assed criminal underworld. And like *American Buffalo*, Lonergan's play concludes with a consideration of male friendship, which trumps family as the major concern of characters caught in this Peter Pan world of extended adolescence.

The play's theme gets punctuated perhaps a bit too hard when Warren, to cover his debts when the drug deal falls apart, is forced to sell his collection of mint-condition toys; Dennis's panicked conversion to sobriety after Stuey's death also seems to me too easy (I thought the author might have been setting up a joke – that Dennis resolves to "totally stop" with drugs every month or so); and the ghost of Warren's sister, meant to provide depth and poignancy to her brother's antics à la *The Catcher in the Rye*, is a bit convenient. But the play's most basic elements are sturdy. And regardless of how pleased David Mamet claims to be with the structure of *American Buffalo*, it is actually the characters and his famous dialogue that form the strength of that play. The same is true here, whether it is Warren explaining to Jessica that he's never been into the cigarette scene himself ("But I hear great things about it") or Dennis putting Warren in his place: "Listen. You're a fuckin' *idiot*. You never have any money. Nobody can stand to have you around. And you can't get laid. I mean, man, you cannot get laid. You *never* get laid."

Dennis is, in fact, a rare creation: a powerful, confident, amoral personality who doesn't seem precious or too adored by the playwright for his naughtiness. Lonergan gives Dennis significant blind spots that undercut his slacker bravado and slyly reflect on the playwright's own hubristic forays away from theater. "I should totally direct movies, man, I'd be a genius at it," Dennis brags. "Like if you take the average person with the average sensibility or sense of humor or the way they look at the world and what thoughts they have or what they think, and you compare it to the way *I* look at shit and the shit I come up with to say, or just the *slant* I put on shit, there's just like no comparison at all. I could totally make movies, man, I would be like one of the greatest movie makers of all time."

As it turns out, *You Can Count on Me* established Lonergan as one of the most intelligent movie makers of recent years. And his two published plays suggest he is one of the few prominent playwrights worthy of significant notice. Though I can't say Lonergan *belongs* in the theater, I would be delighted if he should choose to remain there. Still, if he can continue to produce films of quality equal to his plays, and for a much larger audience, more power to him.

Rebecca Gilman belongs in television. *Boy Gets Girl*, her melodrama about a magazine writer stalked by a near stranger, features a lead character, Theresa, who watches a lot of made-for-T.V. movies in which imperiled women inevitably shoot their relentless attackers. "At first I was disgusted," she admits of her television addiction, "but I found I kept watching the stupid things, because, at the end, I felt this real sense of satisfaction when the stalker got it in the head."

Boy Gets Girl is like a made-for-T.V. movie without an honestly acknowledged formula. Theresa is not attracted to a scoundrel who later shows his true colors. Rather, she is set up on a blind date by a friend who barely knows the guy. Under the circumstances, Theresa has no reason to hold herself accountable when things turn ugly; she possesses no faults (poor judgment, infidelity, a kind heart) that lead to her predicament. Tony, the stalker, simply turns psycho after their first dinner date goes sour. He sends flowers, leaves long telephone messages, shows up at her workplace unannounced, makes violent threats, trashes Theresa's apartment, and finally quits his job so he can dedicate himself full-time to stalking. Tony just exists, like the monster in a horror movie. But this is horror-movie melodrama bereft of suspense: most of the action takes place off-stage, and Tony himself is absent from the entire second act. That leaves room for a lot of scenes examining, commenting on, or illuminating Theresa's plight. But what is there to say? Her plight is bleak.

There are signs that the playwright had more ambitious intentions. "I was wondering," Tony asks Theresa after an early rebuke, "are you afraid of intimacy or something?" The line is meant to put Theresa on the defensive, but Gilman wants us to see more than just Tony's tactical maneuvering. Theresa has no intimate relationships in her life: she hasn't dated in a while, her parents are dead, she maintains no contact with her only sibling, she throws herself into her work. Lack of a personal support network usefully heightens Theresa's sense of isolation and helplessness once Tony's behavior turns threatening, but it also creates an aura of detachment.

It makes sense, then, that Tony fails his first-date audition not by seeming ignorant (he doesn't know who Edith Wharton is) but by opening up emotionally, relating too soon a disaffection for his father and a sense of betrayal by his mother. This is the closest thing Theresa gets to a warning sign that Tony may be willing to chuck his salary and freedom for the chance to intimidate and threaten an unattainable woman. "Most of the time," a policewoman explains to Theresa, "if somebody's being stalked, it's by somebody they had a substantial relationship with. Or a coworker or somebody who sees them every day and has been harboring a secret obsession." Well – not this time. Tony risks going to prison for stalking a woman he has manifestly *not* been obsessing over.

The implications of the play are odd. In the world Gilman sets up, any emotional attachment – indeed, any gesture of sociability a woman makes, no matter how small – leaves her wide open to disruption and dislocation, and to threats of sodomy and murder. This is *Looking for Mr. Goodbar*, minus the sexual moralism. The point gets confused, though, when Theresa is assigned by her editor – against her will – to interview an aging B-movie mogul patterned after Russ Meyer, whose sexploitation films feature unusually large-breasted women. When the film producer, named Les Kennkat, grows impatient with one of Theresa's anecdotes about journalism school, he tries to bring the discussion back into focus and the interview to a close; but Theresa attempts to stall. Later, Les tries in vain to cut off their relationship ("I don't want you writing anything about me") and Theresa counters with creepy insistence ("Well, you can't stop me").

We are meant to register the dichotomy between Theresa's role in the professional world (stalker) and its reversal in the private world (victim), but to what end? Further confusing matters is the reading Theresa's male colleagues give her article on the lecherous Kennkat: it's about Tony and Theresa, they conclude. It illustrates how men are trained to view women as objects, and how women are trained to accept that role. (They've got the Theresa-Kennkat relationship reversed here, or the playwright has, but what follows from this mix-up remains undetermined.)

A narrative about a stalker, it seems to me, has two options, neither of which is particularly promising. The play can observe how simple it is for one person to violate another's security, or if the stalker is a man, it can emphasize the special vulnerability of women. If the author pursues the second option, she runs the risk of downplaying female aggression and ignoring the experience of every closeted gay man I've known (of being stalked, harassed, and groped by women, from junior high on). Gilman acknowledges Theresa's aggressive side, but in a fitful way that she ultimately nullifies. The other elements of the play – Tony's abrupt personality change, Theresa's unaccountable bad luck, the obediently crude or sympathetic secondary characters – release a veritable tsunami of feminist self-righteousness that drowns all gestures toward depth or complexity.

Particularly unfortunate is the playwright's handling of Les Kennkat and Madeleine Beck, the police officer working on Theresa's case. Leering and vulgar, Kennkat is an unimaginative caricature who talks the way male actors do in pornographic movies. This is precisely how dull women who would bother to get upset over Russ Meyer's obscure, campy films might imagine Russ Meyer. Officer Beck, on the other hand, is all business until she recounts how her parents gave her five brothers a free ride through college, but never offered to pay for her education. She concludes her story by giving Theresa "a big hug." This surprises Theresa, but she relaxes and accepts the gesture.

Sisterhood, then, succeeds in cracking the armor of emotional detachment. Already in the early 1980s, the comediennes on *SCTV* were skewering this sort of earnest narrative in a merciless theater satire titled, if memory serves, *I'm Taking My Own Head, Screwing It on Right, and No Guy's Gonna Tell Me That It Ain't*. In their final scene, Andrea Martin and Catherine O'Hara meet downstage in a tearful, triumphant embrace, while Joe Flaherty, their erstwhile romantic interest, hovers artfully upstage, hanging from a gallows. Gilman doesn't realize it, but Theresa and Officer Beck belong in an anti-feminist parody of this ilk, or in a depthless television world where men always have it coming and women can count on getting their violent revenge.

Gilman's previous play, *Spinning into Butter*, premiered at the Goodman Theatre in Chicago and was subsequently produced at Lincoln Center in New York City. One got the impression from the buzz surrounding these projects that, if *Boy Gets Girl* was sanctimonious, *Spinning into Butter* was inflammatory, dangerous, almost downright irresponsible. This turns out to be true, but in a paradoxically safe way. For all the apparent controversy, Gilman isn't one to act brashly; she spoonfeeds her audience.

Spinning into Butter is set in the office of Sarah Daniels, Dean of Students at Belmont College, a bucolic New England institution. When an African-American student finds racist notes tacked on the door to his dormitory room, faculty and students alike react with indignation and facile soul-searching. "If we handle this right, it could be a real learning experience for the students," notes one instructor. Race forums and discussion groups are held.

Gilman has moved into A.R. Gurney territory here. (One student suggests instituting a student group on tolerance, which he can take credit for on his law school applications.) The playwright convincingly mocks the petty agendas of academics. But the faculty members, while conniving, are not very savvy. As an investigation gets underway, no one asks the obvious questions: Has the victim made any personal enemies on campus? Might the whole incident be a hoax?

By the time Sarah Daniels voices her belief that the brouhaha among her white colleagues is some sort of cheap penance, we are ready for the racial episode to serve as just one element in a play about something larger – but what? The obtuseness of intellectuals? The opportunism of self-declared victims? The arrogance of youths raised by baby-boomers? Nearly every university faculty member I know views today's undergraduates with a certain skepticism, if not disdain. Yet Sarah is unquestioningly cowed by a nasty-tempered student from New York City whose family is Puerto Rican. She offers him a minority scholarship; he accepts, them berates her for the demeaning categorization, which she in turn sincerely apologizes for. Neither liberal guilt nor the missionary zeal of a college administrator can account persuasively for her abjectly spineless behavior.

As it turns out, Sarah worked previously at a traditionally African-American college in Chicago. Unhappy in that situation, she fled to Vermont to escape working primarily with black students. "It made me worse," she tells a colleague of her own experience as a numerical minority. "I mean, before I started there, I was just paternalistic. Now I'm fully aware that black people have agency and are responsible and can help themselves, but I think they don't do it because they're lazy and stupid."

Her full confession runs fifteen pages in the published script. It may not clearly explain why Sarah lets a white student of Puerto Rican heritage bully her into submission. (Like the female undergraduate in David Mamet's *Oleanna*, this "Nuyorican" male is presented in such a way that would make brutal rejection seem too generous.) But Sarah's self-defensive tirade is legitimately eye-opening, and Gilman deserves credit for going out on a limb.

But only partial credit. For every line of Sarah's self-incriminating honesty there is a bit of backtracking ("There were plenty of nice kids"). Worse, the playwright interjects correctives from Sarah's colleague in a severely misguided attempt at ideological balance, the effect of which is to sabotage the dramatic moment. "But you were encountering them after years and years of privation and discrimination," he informs her – *us* – in the boring, implausible language of a dramaturgical mouthpiece. "After an economic and educational system had utterly failed them."

Gilman takes other missteps. For example, one character makes a long, forced analogy between this story and the Little Black Sambo fable, an insistence meant to justify the play's title. Ultimately, though, the drama is done in by leaving us just where we began, with the same unrattled sense of our enlightenment and virtue. Gilman expects us to take away from the play the same simplistic truths we bring to it: no person is representative of an entire race, no one can speak for an entire race. Why is contemporary American drama so bad? Because playwrights are regularly rewarded for aiming so low.

[2002]

Oppositional Playwrights, Conformist Views

The unifying question in David Savran's second collection of interviews with American playwrights, *The Playwright's Voice* (TCG, 1999), concerns the renewed importance of ghosts on the contemporary stage. "I am tempted to read our monsters allegorically, as the materialization of new anxieties," instructs Savran in his introduction. Those anxieties arise from the spread of chemical, biological, and nuclear weapons and the proliferation of localized wars following the collapse of the Soviet Union. Phantom characters in Tony Kushner's *Angel in America*, Paula Vogel's *How I Learned to Drive*, and other works also imply renewed interest in the occult and spirituality, Savran explains. Moreover, the American stage at the end of the twentieth century is haunted by the very idea of America.

Savran admits, however, that ghosts have populated the stage from ancient Greek tragedy through Renaissance drama and on up to *Our Town*, *Death of a Salesman*, and other early- and mid-twentieth century works. And his assertion that the unipolar world of the 1990's generated greater anxiety than did the tense bipolar world of the Cold War is suspect. In the collection's first interview, Edward Albee takes issue with Savran over his suggestion that we are witnessing an explosion of ghostly figures on stage. Undaunted, Savran emphasizes the theory throughout the remaining fourteen conversations.

By so doing, Savran overlooks obvious aesthetic and practical considerations. Theater has always featured ghosts because they are a cheap way to spook the audience (*Hamlet*) and they help dramatize the conflicted psychology of the protagonists (*Macbeth*). In a novel, the narrative can shift seamlessly into past tense, but a play is limited to undramatic exposition, unsequential scenes, or ghostlike revisitings. And with economic restrictions usually limiting cast size to five actors or fewer, there is a terrible temptation to keep a newly deceased character onstage and talking: the producer has already paid the actor for an entire evening's work.

Saddam Hussein and his store of weapons of mass destruction may have less to do with the current vogue of theatrical ghosts – in indeed there is one – than do the limitations of stagecraft, but Savran, a professor of English at Brown University, chooses not to consider stagecraft here. Instead, he examines theater through the lens of politics. Like most drama critics, Savran honors playwrights less as craftsmen or artists than as rebels – contrarians who, like academics, shun the commercial enticements of Hollywood and other lucrative media bases. "[T]he most honored and well-known playwrights – from Williams, Miller and Albee to Kushner and Vogel – have invariably acquired their renown in part by challenging received opinions," Savran observes. Yet Kushner's most admired work, *Angels in America*, is a catalogue of received opinions: Roy Cohn was a fascinating yet morally repulsive human being, Ethel Rosenberg was an innocent martyr, religions oppress and dupe even while they build community, Ronald Reagan exacerbated the toll from AIDS. Kushner's characters shout a lot – they *sound* like they're saying something controversial – but they are reporting what an educated urban audience expects to hear. Those met expectations, rather than the play's perceived daring, may account for Kushner's success.

Indeed, the central irony of the contemporary drama business is that one can establish credentials as an oppositional figure by espousing conformist views. Savran reports that, taking identity politics for granted, the new generation of playwrights deals with questions of sexuality, race, and gender with a frankness and combativeness that were unimaginable forty years ago. But by taking identity politics "for granted," members of the new generation permit received opinion to go unchallenged, and their hand-me-down concerns may account for the waning interest in American theater that a number of the playwrights lament.

Still, Savran elicits a fair amount of good sense from the younger writers. Nicky Silver, asked if he considers his own work subversive, replies: "Not remotely. [...] I don't think it's possible to be subversive anymore, certainly not in the theater. [...] There are certain things you could do on stage that would shock people. The problem is, you wouldn't get produced, and if you did, it would be preaching to the converted."

Other playwrights offer sharp, honest observations as well. Anna Deavere Smith, who performs in her own pieces, notes how the stagy quality of contemporary conversation impedes her work. "We don't talk from a truthful place," she laments, "we talk from a performative place, which makes our work as actors very hard because we're living in a society where everyone's acting." Mac Wellman admits to keeping a notebook of ideas for plays, but he insists that a work of art should be unparaphrasable. "So I don't generally write, 'I want to write a play about the problem of ...' Because it would then make the most sense to write an article about it, to cut to the quick and get the matter over with." And Suzan-Lori Parks reports she has had to save productions from directors who felt that all theater should be weird and avant-garde and abstract: "I guess that's fine if the play is well known like *Hamlet*," she allows. "But newer plays should be seen in an imaginative way, in a way that makes them pop, but not in a way that obscures them."

Parks's observations echo stinging comments by Edward Albee in defense of the script. Albee rebuts Savran's contention that a produced play is – yes – a *ghost*, in that the written text is dead and must be brought to life on stage. "I don't think plays are made any better by performance," Albee scolds. "A good production finds all sorts of things embedded in the text, but a bad production distorts by imposing outside stuff. It's that simple."

Numerous writers comment here on the health of the American theater, but no consensus is reached. Savran contrasts the gloom he observed a decade ago when preparing his previous collection of interviews, *In Their Own Words* (1988), with what he considers the renaissance of American theater today. Paula Vogel concurs. "I'm not worried about the theater dying," she says, convinced small companies will flourish. But Albee and Kushner sense regional theater is approaching its demise. And Wendy Wasserstein, whose plays appear regularly on Broadway, fears for the survival of American theater in general.

Pessimists and optimists alike consider National Endowment for the Arts funding crucial to the survival of theater, and they may be right, but few of them address the issue honestly. Most conflate censorship with a threatened cut in federal subsidies. An exception is Nicky Silver, who admits, "I don't know what gives me the right to say, 'You have to give me money,' if you don't want to." Silver seems willing to let politics and the marketplace take their toll, and his fatalism is a breath of fresh air amid the generally panicked self-promotion of this collection. Of course, the sort of plays Silver writes – consisting, as he says, of five characters and a bare stage – is the least likely to disappear. "It's the big spectacle play that will be gone," he notes. "So if it goes, it goes."

[2000]

TONY KUSHNER TALKING

In 1994, Tony Kushner premiered *Slavs! (Thinking About the Longstanding Problems of Virtue and Happiness)*. Set primarily in 1985, the play features among its characters Aleksii Antedilluvianovich Prelapsarianov – late of *Angels in America* – and a handful of fellow Kremlin habitués who fret among themselves over the difficulty of proceeding without a viable political theory. In reality, it is highly unlikely any true believer set foot in the Kremlin after the show trials of the 1930s. Compounding that absurdity, Kushner opens the play with a prologue featuring a pair of babushkas discussing the conditions of social development in rigidly Marxist terms.

Clearly, the author is projecting his vocabulary and obsessions onto his characters, who in reality would know better. One can gaze in disbelief at the playwright's naïveté or look away in embarrassment. But one cannot ignore Tony Kushner forever. The worldwide success of *Angels in America* has illuminated him; he is one of the bright stars in the theatrical constellation. Nor can one disregard his political convictions. They are expounded in his plays, essays, and numerous published interviews, twenty-one of which are selected by Robert Vorlicky for inclusion in *Tony Kushner in Conversation* (University of Michigan Press, 1998).

Vorlicky's book covers the years 1990 to 1997, when Kushner's basic beliefs were challenged by the collapse of the Soviet Union. Blind to the accumulated rot of the Communist system – the inefficiency and corruption endemic to a command economy – Kushner was thrown for a loop by the events of 1989 and 1991. Even so, he retains ultimate allegiance to the utopian premise of Marxism. As he explains to Craig Lucas: "The idea of socialism is still completely valid, and the collapse of the Soviet system doesn't in any way mean that capitalism has succeeded. [...] Socialism is simply the idea that people are better off if we work collectively and that the economic system we live in is made by people and therefore can be controlled intelligently rather than let loose. There's no way that can't be true."

Obviously, Kushner is befuddled by paradox. This is no small weakness in a writer. But the facts remain: an economic scheme boasting an attractive egalitarian premise will likely serve its citizens poorly and collapse, while another, fueled by self-interest and profit, might serve its citizens well and thrive. Furthermore, a political system posing as the savior of the working class may prove to be its genocidal tormentor while a seemingly indifferent rival assumes the roles of benefactor and protector. There is an abundance of folk wisdom to guide us here: "actions speak louder than words," for example; or "he can talk the talk, but can he walk the walk." Unfortunately, a political system's packaging often takes precedence among artists and intellectuals. In *"The Russian Question" At the End of the Twentieth Century*, Alexander Solzhenitsyn observes, "Soviet diplomacy was furnished with such ideologically attractive plumage that it won the rapturous sympathy of the *progressive society* in the West" (dismayed emphasis his). Far longer than almost anyone else, Kushner allowed to linger a rapturous sympathy, if not for the Soviet Union as it was, then for an idealized system yet to be imposed over the decomposing Stalinist model. I seem to be alone among dramatists and drama critics in finding this to Tony Kushner's discredit.

Kushner set his first major work, *A Bright Room Called Day* (1987), in Weimar Germany. Its twenty-five primary scenes plus a prologue and epilogue move along at a decent clip. The problem, as everyone who comments on the play notes, is the eight didactic interruptions made by an anachronistic American character named Zillah, who detects ominous parallels between the rise of the National Socialists and Ronald Reagan's irrepressible popularity. Throughout his published interviews, Kushner devotes considerable energy to refuting criticism of Zillah and of her inflammatory accusations. He shares her views, he insists, and they are legitimate. More generally, he states: "I firmly believe in using the Holocaust model, promiscuously. I think we should be very liberal with likening people to Nazis." Yet in the play's published text, the author greases his exit. Zillah is not the playwright, he emphasizes in the production notes. And in the afterword he admits: "It is immature, certainly, to write a play which asks an audience, among other things, to consider comparisons between Ronald Reagan and Adolf Hitler. *A Bright Room Called Day* is an immature play."

The problems with Zillah's scenes are not limited to the playwright's immaturity. To paraphrase Truman Capote, these scenes are improper – not morally, aesthetically. "You tax the audience every time you don't move on to the next essential step of the progression as quickly as possible," David Mamet has observed of the dramatic process. "You're taxing their good nature." If the audience indulges you, it does so for purely political reasons.

Tony Kushner expects to be indulged – endlessly – for purely political reasons. This grows wearisome, here and in *Angels in America*, a work, like Toni Morrison's *Beloved*, that one feels bullied into admiring. Public dissent is not permitted. As Vorlicky observes, Kushner has been "bear-hugged by the media," and Deborah R. Geis and Steven F. Kruger suggest in their introduction to *Approaching the Millennium: Essays on Angels in America* that the hyperbolic praise the plays have received has itself been transformed into an object of admiration and scorn.

I'm convinced this playwright's success originates from his dramatic works. (His interviews suggest he is no PR expert.) But his plays have serious problems with pacing, tone, structure, and – most important – vision. Perhaps these are problems endemic to big works, but I can't ignore them. Kushner's artistic house will remain a mess until he ceases to lecture, procrastinate, and shine a spotlight of glory upon himself under the guise of drama.

Kushner might choose to defend all this as merely one facet of his homosexual fabulousness – *fabulous* being a term he applies liberally to his gay characters, his work, or any aspect of gay life that doesn't hold up well under scrutiny but which Kushner is loathe to repudiate. There are, in fact, considerable incidental pleasures to be had from *Angels in America*, particularly in the first two acts of

Part One, Millennium Approaches. The main characters are exceptionally well realized: Roy Cohn, of course; the Mormon law clerk, Joe Pitt, his agoraphobic wife, Harper, and his mother, Hannah; Louis and Prior, a disintegrating gay couple; and Belize, a registered nurse who treats both Prior and Roy Cohn for AIDS. And there is at least one great theatrical moment, in scene seven of act one, when Prior appears in Harper's Valium-induced hallucination and she invades his illness-related dream. But the energy goes out of the narrative during the first four meandering scenes of act three, killing the play's momentum, which never recovers in *Part Two, Perestroika*.

In his 1995 essay "On Pretentiousness," Kushner admits to an attraction to grand gestures and histrionics. "A good play I think should always feel as though it's only barely been rescued from the brink of chaos," he writes, "[...] from the mess it might just as easily have been." In an interview that same year with Susan Jonas, he claims Herman Melville as a favorite author. "[P]art of what I adore about him is that he makes it *a trope* to be oversized and outrageous and much bigger than anyone could possibly be. [...] Of course it's going to collapse under its own weight. But isn't it great that we're doing this?" By championing his weaknesses, Kushner can refute any criticism leveled at his work. To Leo Bersani's charge that *Angels in America* is muddled and pretentious, for example, he responds: "Muddled and pretentious are I think among the plays' charms."

The production notes to *A Bright Room Called Day* state, "Editing is possible throughout, and recommended." From one point of view, this is rather admirable and unpossessive of the author. But one could insist the playwright has an obligation to hone his manuscript and assemble its scenes in a definitive way that makes *ad hoc* editing unnecessary. *Angels in America* suffers from a problem more critical than mere sluggishness or disorder, however. I refer to the author's effort to orchestrate a gay self-righteousness rivaling in urgency the Jewish response to the Holocaust. "It's about people being trapped in systems that they didn't participate in creating," Kushner tells Tom Szentgyorgyi in 1990, and it is unclear which work he is referring to: his two-part epic about Americans battling AIDS or his earlier play about Germans fighting the onslaught of the Nazis. By featuring an infamously vile Republican among his cast of characters, by making unequal access to trial medications central to his plot, and by associating the general heterosexual indifference toward AIDS with, of all things, McCarthyism, Kushner would like to suggest that Ronald Reagan and George Bush are, in his own words, "as morally debased as the people who followed Hitler." Kushner tells Craig Lucas in 1993, "So much of what we've lived through in the last twelve years has shown us that these people really are murderers. They're very, very, very evil people." And he spells it out more clearly for Patrick R. Pacheco, claiming that for gay men who have dodged the AIDS bullet, "it's really like Holocaust survivors have to think about it." Finally, in response to the 1994 election of a Republican-controlled Congress, Kushner writes: "[I]t is no exaggeration to say that as a direct result of laws and amendments [that] these criminally reckless, criminally stupid, mendacious neo-barbarians are enacting, millions of people will die."

"He is cordial and sensitive to those whose opinions are different from his," Robert Vorlicky writes of Kushner in his introduction. Such a statement bears witness to the vulnerability of academics, journalists, and activists to a playwright who pulls no punches and who offers in his character Prior – a sick and lonely yet fabulous gay man – someone who has caught not a sexually transmitted disease but, rather, "the virus of prophesy." You don't need to study Freud to grasp the dynamic at work here: desperate efforts to project the onus for AIDS onto persons and institutions associated with conventional sexual morality have reached a pitch of hysteria. "Shrillness is not a sign of intellect," Harold Brodkey once wrote. "Or of judgment. (It usually indicates bad nerves and a weak vocabulary and limited powers of reason.)" Yet Kushner's admirers insist on interpreting his shrillness as a sign of intellect or, worse, claim it is not shrillness at all but is, in fact, respectful discourse.

"I'm just not interested in universal human truths," Kushner tells Michael Lowenthal. "I'm interested in politics." In "On Pretentiousness," he writes: "To make overtly political art you must, I think, always declare more than you can prove and say more than you can know." It's no surprise, then, that Kushner has a glib answer for everything: What accounts for the relative obscurity of Latina playwright Maria Irene Fornes? Racism. What has led to the increasing incidence of breast cancer? Sexism, misogyny. Why do drug companies conduct double-blind medication trials? Stupidity and homophobia. What spurred the catastrophic spread of AIDS? Well, nothing to do with demographic shifts or viral mutation or sexual exposure or persistent risk-taking during periods of inebriation – nothing, that is, that would allow the truth to impinge on Kushner's politics. Like many gay ideologues, Kushner takes an unapologetically Marcusean approach to most issues. He doesn't permit the evidence to shape his views; rather, his views shape the evidence. Thus, his answer to the question of how AIDS cut such a wide swath through the gay community can be reduced to two words: Ronald Reagan.

This is unfortunate for many reasons, but chiefly because there is a legitimate case to be made against recent administrations for neglecting to lead more forcefully the national and international response to AIDS. But building such a case would preclude further misuse of the word *genocide*; it would require sophisticated interpretation of statistical evidence; and it might in the end suggest that research on AIDS, by the same objective criteria that implicate Ronald Reagan, is now overfunded relative to other scourges like heart disease and malaria. But I fear such a case could never be made in the current political environment that Kushner has helped to shape.

"I had to write a piece about 'Sex in the Time of the Plague' recently for *Esquire*," Kushner tells Patrick R. Pacheco, "and my first take was, 'Everybody should go out and have as much sex as they can get.' And then I read about the San Francisco study showing a sharp increase in HIV rates among young gay men. And so I reconsidered my position." It must be said of Kushner that he faces a very steep learning curve for someone his age, in economics, in sexual ecology – well, in every field, but these are the two he stumbles around in most often. Like many writers who embrace a politics promising unconditional sexual liberation, Kushner misunderstands the character and origins of sexual morality. It is not some arbitrary irritant cooked up by a dozen grumpy men sitting in a room. Rather, it is one of many awkward weapons a culture wields against nature, superintended by a Darwinian process of selection. I'm not suggesting people should dutifully acquiesce to their culture's sexual regulations. But I must insist that artists, intellectuals, and activists stop ignoring inconvenient facts for reasons of ideological expediency.

Kushner considers sexually adventurous gay men participants in a politically legitimate experiment, but he admits there are biological problems associated with unfettered sexual activity. When the epidemic came along, "we" – he means homosexuals – "lost a tremendous amount of daring and courage and the power to imagine what was possible. And one must grieve for that." More precisely, what was lost with the advent of AIDS – in addition to lives – was the folly to assume possible that which was clearly impossible. A subculture that conducts a sexual experiment across several continents and emerges unscathed is as likely as a centrally planned economy that avoids corruption. As noted, Kushner has trouble handling paradox. He fails to acknowledge the dystopian character of utopian revelations, the dual nature of which has been clear since Sir Thomas More coined the term *utopia* nearly 500 years ago and imagined his own ideal society: a creepy, lockstep culture in which possessions were communally owned. The author who emerges from *Tony Kushner in Conversation* is an advocate for an economic system that leads to impoverishment, a retroactive cheerleader for a sexual experiment that went awry and caused untold death and suffering, and an attack dog against anyone who, on practical grounds, takes issue with his foolish utopian schemes.

In the epilogue to *Slavs!*, the character Vodya Domik summarizes her despair as the Soviet system implodes around her. She wonders if visionary objectives – "social justice, economic justice, equality, community" – are simply unenforceable, and if there is no alternative to capitalism but Stalinism, the gulags, and the death of free thought. But Vodya Domik is not the playwright. Elsewhere, Kushner reiterates his approval – "at least in theory" – of the sort of doomed system Vodya Domik sees collapsing before her eyes. In the process, Kushner claims for himself the highest attributes: virtue, moral seriousness, intellectual curiosity, generosity. At one time, these attributes had to be earned. I fear their acquisition through self-declaration is a sign of where our culture at large is heading – to the same irrational place where the commissars of contemporary gay culture have long resided: the land of the fabulous.

[2000]

Direct Solicitation to Agent

Nearly every playwright across the country who wishes to attract a producer consults a publication of the Theater Communications Group titled *Dramatists Sourcebook*. It lists the names and addresses of most of the country's well-established regional theaters and notes their submission procedures. What the aspiring playwright hopes to find under the latter category is "accepts unsolicited scripts." But he is more likely to see "no unsolicited scripts; accepts synopsis and letter of inquiry." And all too often he is foiled by "direct solicitation to agent." Perusing *Dramatists Sourcebook* one notices that almost every major metropolitan area outside New York City boasts one or two major theater companies entirely removed from the business of developing writing talent. Instead, they stage Broadway and Off-Broadway hits of the past season or two, priding themselves on bringing the finest of contemporary American theater to the hinterlands. Some of these companies don't bother to list themselves in *Dramatists Sourcebook* at all — what would be the point? They know what they want, and they know where to get it.

I reside in one of many cities where the three plays under review, all of which have enjoyed lengthy New York runs, will be staged this season, procured no doubt through direct solicitation to agent. Their regional productions coincide with their publication in trade paperback, the method by which contemporary American theater truly reaches the hinterlands – the vast areas outside the reach of even the regional circuit. Such was certainly the case when I was growing up. The local "troupe" importing recent Broadway fare was our public library. Plays were read, not staged, or so I came to believe. And it is with that skewed mindset that I still approach most dramatic texts.

Alfred Uhry, author of *Driving Miss Daisy*, has written a second play destined to strike regional-theater gold, falling as it does into two of the most oft-repeated Special Interest categories listed in *Dramatists Sourcebook*: 1) "comedies that appeal to a general audience" and 2) "plays addressing socially relevant and/or minority issues." Uhry, who collects prizes and awards – Pulitzer, Oscar, and for this play Tony – has returned to the mid-century milieu of upper-middle-class Atlanta Jews to tell a story of husband hunting and anti-Semitism among Semites.

Set in December 1939, the week of *Gone with the Wind's* film premiere and a time of ominous developments in Europe, *The Last Night of Ballyhoo* (TCG, 1997) offers an affectionate view of an extended German-Jewish family whose only flaw is a lingering, largely benign prejudice against Jews of Slavic and Hungarian descent. The family is somewhat estrogen-heavy, consisting of a sole male, Adolph (get it?) Freitag, his widowed sister Boo, their widowed sister-in-law Reba, plus Boo's emotionally immature adult daughter Lala and, when she's not at college, Reba's brainy daughter Sunny. Both daughters are of marrying age. This provokes a competitive spirit in the girl cousins who it seems have always been at odds, growing up close in age but with dissimilar appearance and demeanor. Sunny is the pretty, well-adjusted one who rises above the petty concerns of

Atlanta society, while Lala, who considers herself more "Jewish-looking," clings to the old ways and is willing to elevate her own position at the expense of her non-German brethren.

Sunny's visit home for the holidays coincides with Ballyhoo, a social event that draws young, unmarried German Jews from across the South, and culminates in a formal dance. Lala is beside herself trying to find a date, and sets her sights on Joe Farkas, her uncle's young business assistant, who wears his East European ethnicity and his Jewish heritage too openly for some in the Freitag family, who are embarrassed neither by the Christmas tree in their living room nor their sketchy familiarity with the tradition of Passover Seder. Lala's mother has an ideal suitor in mind for her daughter: the mysterious, unseen Sylvan "Peachy" Weil from Lake Charles.

We know where this is heading, or we think we do: Lala will find herself ultimately crushed and further enfeebled emotionally, like Laura in *The Glass Menagerie*, unable to bear even the rigors of typing class. But as it turns out the play's most explosive conflict concerns Joe, who fails to realize until he is at the Ballyhoo dance that the arbiters of privilege are allowing him only temporary access to the inner sanctum of elite Jewish society. Some have criticized as inappropriate or superficial the parallels Uhry draws between the exclusionary snobbery of some of the Atlanta Jews and the genocidal campaign then in the planning stages in Germany. My only objection is to the ease with which the play's conflict is resolved.

In an interview, Lanford Wilson, author of the plays *The Hot L Baltimore* and *Fifth of July* among others, confessed that he "gooses" his plays by creating characters who are "far-out" and "wacky" in order to emphasize the work's "theatricality." I can think of nothing more unsavory than watching an actor attempt to deliver an inorganically wacky character. Here, the wacky character is clearly sister-in-law Reba who, when her niece runs from the room distraught from her mother's harping, states blankly, "Poor thing. I think she must be constipated." But this being an Alfred Uhry play, Reba is only mildly wacky. I've thus far resisted the urge to use the word "tepid" to describe *The Last Night of Ballyhoo*, but I'm afraid I must now submit. But tepid can be fine too. (Some playwrights would be well advised to ungoose their work with a few tepid characters.) The play features an attractive family, concerns young love, and is set in a time when mothers advised daughters "to prepare some peppy and interesting topics to discuss." I must confess I find such an atmosphere irresistible. For that, I may epitomize the general audience referred to in *Dramatists Sourcebook*.

The biographical statement at the back of Paula Vogel's book *The Mammary Plays* (TCG, 1998) lists among the theaters where the author's works have been performed the Goodman Theatre in Chicago and the Alley Theatre in Houston (both "professional recommendation"), the American Repertory Theatre in Cambridge, Massachusetts ("agent submission"), and Baltimore's Center Stage and the Magic Theatre in San Francisco ("no unsolicited scripts"). By far, Vogel's most successful effort to date is *How I Learned to Drive*, which ran for a year Off-Broadway and is in the works at no fewer than fifty theaters around the country.

At recent talks and during interviews she gave upon receiving the Pulitzer Prize, Vogel made a number of revealing statements about *How I Learned to Drive* and playwriting in general. She explained that she set out in this play to rewrite *Lolita* from the girl's perspective, without demonizing the character Peck, the incestuous uncle of the main character, Li'l Bit. Demonizing, she felt, left no room for transcendence. She also concurred with Aristotle's point that, in the end, it's a play's structure not its language that determines if a production will soar or stumble.

That point pertains to *How I Learned to Drive*, with its not entirely authentic dialogue and its weaving time structure that ultimately arrives where it must to bring resonance to the story. This structural triumph is accomplished in spite of the fact that the author has saddled the narrative with the running conceit, tied to the title, of announcing the start of each scene with a quote from a drivers education film: "You and the Reverse Gear," "When Making a Left Turn, You Must Downshift While Going Forward," "Vehicle Failure," and so on. Could this be intended as the play's "wacky" element? Li'l Bit's opening line of dialogue is, "Sometimes to tell a secret, you first have to teach a lesson." This statement made no more sense to me after finishing the play than it did at first reading.

In addition to the actors playing Li'l Bit and Peck, there are three other cast members, designated the Greek Chorus by the author, who play a number of family members and other roles. Vogel doesn't demonize Uncle Peck, who is plagued by memories of battle in World War II, who drinks, and who Li'l Bit speculates may himself have been molested as a child. But the rest of the family – Li'l Bit's mother and grandmother, who discuss female orgasms at the kitchen table, her grandfather and Aunt Mary – are quite awful. Li'l Bit aspires to rise above her "cracker background," believing crackers are naturally destined for hell, but she cannot exorcise her own crackerness completely: at one point she improbably describes the university she briefly attended on scholarship as "that fancy school." I found the atmospherics of the dialogue a problem elsewhere as well, but Vogel is right: it's not a play's language but rather its structure that ultimately brings a narrative to a gripping conclusion.

I deliberately withheld information about the final scenes of *The Last Night of Ballyhoo* because it is a simple story and one's enjoyment of the play would be lessened by knowing everything beforehand. In contrast, *How I Learned to Drive* has a slippery, perplexing premise that cannot be "ruined." There is a cost to the author for not demonizing Peck: one can come away with a nebulous sense of her point of view, at least upon first exposure to the play. It will therefore do no harm – and may help – if I reveal here how the play ends.

In the third-to-last scene, a forty-five-year-old Peck – on good behavior of late, off the bottle, and waiting patiently until Li'l Bit's eighteenth birthday when statutory rape laws no longer apply – proposes marriage to his niece (they are not blood relatives). Li'l Bit refuses, at which point Peck turns fetal and asks for a drink. Within seven years, we are told, Peck will drink himself to death.

In the penultimate scene, it is seven years earlier, and we see what has set everything in motion: Uncle Peck, under the guise of teaching his eleven-year-old niece to drive a car, fondles her in his lap, bringing himself to orgasm.

And, finally, with Uncle Peck ten years dead, a thirty-five-year-old Li'l Bit finds herself accepting things – "like family and forgiveness" – that her younger self would never have allowed. We hear an echo of an earlier line of Uncle Peck's dialogue – "I have loved you since the day I held you in my hand" – a sentiment offered as evidence of their special relationship, but which suggests here the possibility of breeding relatives for sex. But time has passed, perspective has been gained, and bitterness has receded. At play's end, Li'l Bit looks into her rearview mirror, sees the ghost of Uncle Peck, and smiles.

Like *How I Learned to Drive*, Martin McDonagh's Broadway hit *The Beauty Queen of Leenane* (Vintage, 1998) features a white trash family – this one Irish – and a brilliantly structured narrative. The main difference is the additional element of genius – that is, McDonagh's. This young Anglo-Irish playwright has clearly been blessed by the gods.

The Beauty Queen of Leenane might appear at first glance to be the sort of domestic tragedy theaters in *Dramatists Sourcebook* abhor. "No kitchen sink dramas" states one theater after another. In fact, the kitchen sink plays a central role in the plot. Set in the bleakest corner of County Galway, in the (almost) present, the play features an elderly mother, Mag, and her resentful virgin daughter, the forty-year-old Maureen, who trade barbs and generally make each other's isolated lives miserable. It wasn't entirely clear to me from reading the play if the dynamic between clutching mother and unappreciated daughter is intended to be played as primarily bleak, humorous, campy à la *What Ever Happened to Baby Jane?*, or some combination thereof. The author has set their remote house at the top of a hill, which Mag cannot navigate alone, and which neighbors, even the young and sprightly, have no interest in climbing. Her dependence on her daughter, then, is complete, though the dynamics of their master-slave relationship are fluid.

In Scene Two of the first act, one of those neighbors, young Ray Dooley, makes the climb to the house to invite the two women to a "do" in honor of his uncle. He's been sent on the errand by his older brother, Pato – a former acquaintance of Maureen's who has worked off and on in England for the past twenty years. Ray leaves behind a note, which Mag, fearful of any personal relationship that might lure her daughter away, burns. When Maureen returns to the house from her chores, she asks disingenuously if anyone has stopped by. (She met Ray on his way out and received the invitation firsthand.) Her mother tells her no.

The mechanics of the rest of the plot are foreshadowed in that early scene. Foreshadowed elsewhere is the family's potential for violence. When Maureen later talks to Pato, she asks him about two local brothers, one of whom has clipped off the other's dog's ears out of spite. In Pato's presence, Mag accuses Maureen of deliberately scalding her hand. And in the very first scene, Mag expresses dismay at the story of a Dubliner who murdered a complete stranger, an elderly woman.

MAUREEN: Sure, that sounds like the type of fella I would like to meet, and then bring him home to meet you, if he likes murdering oul women.
MAG: That's not a nice thing to say, Maureen.
MAUREEN: Is it not, now?
MAG: (*pause*) Sure why would he be coming all this way out from Dublin? He'd just be going out of his way.
MAUREEN: For the pleasure of keeping me company he'd come. Killing you, it'd just be a bonus for him.
MAG: Killing you I bet he first would be.
MAUREEN: I could live with that so long as I was sure he'd be clobbering you soon after.

What helps make this morbid exchange and others like it a delight to the ear is, of course, the (invented?) Galwegian dialect, which to the unacquainted ear sounds musical, with its unusual syntax ("Killing you I bet he first would be"). It brightens scenes that would otherwise simply entail two hideous women bickering. But the women remain hideous nevertheless.

When a writer creates such a spectacle, he is obviously commenting on the nature of God. But he is also assuming God's place, and as a divinity, McDonagh is not very generous toward his creations. He is, however, generous toward the audience, sharing his gifts for character, dialogue, and plot, the elements of which pass the classic test: they are unpredictable, yet seem immediately inevitable. Even the scene that everyone knows is coming – a repeat of Scene Two where Ray leaves behind another note with Mag – is milked for as much tension as possible. The play's underlying theme – that the families we are born into may turn grotesque and prevent us from starting a family of our own – may not seem especially urgent, but there's a universal quality to it. I was reminded of the historical books of the Old Testament, with their improbably violent and pornographic stories of dysfunctional families and clans. Insistent Irish friends inform me that a good number of the American musical forms – bluegrass, folk, country – descend directly from traditional Irish music. Now another Irish influence has been revealed: the Irish were the first crackers.

[1998]

Hot New Plays!

Last summer, the Studio Theatre in Washington, D.C., commenced its advertising campaign for the coming season. Following works by Britons Tom Stoppard, Caryl Churchill, Harold Pinter, and South African Athol Fugard, the lone American entry was to be *Side Man*, the recent Broadway success by Warren Leight. Within a few weeks, however, Studio's advertisements changed, touting *Hot New Play!* as its fifth offering. The theater had to scramble to replace *Side Man* because the national touring company of Leight's drama was now scheduled to visit the Kennedy Center in November, preempting Studio's planned May 2000 opening.

The Studio Theatre announced its final revised schedule during *Side Man*'s Kennedy Center run, unexpectedly replacing Pinter's *Betrayal* with *Bash*, a collection of related one-acts by American filmmaker Neil Labute, and concluding with Christopher Durang's most recent New York premiere, *Betty's Summer Vacation*. American chauvinists could now relax: not only had their countrymen not been wiped completely off the Studio schedule, they had inexplicably gained a spot.

Side Man (Grove, 1998) had previously carried the weight of the author's nationality on its shoulders in New York where it competed for tourist dollars and industry awards against a number of foreign plays and a British production of Tennessee Williams's *Not About Nightingales*. Like Williams's *Glass Menagerie*, *Side Man* is a memory play, narrated by the twenty-nine-year-old son of a jazz trumpeter and his estranged, deranged wife. There are also traces of the BBC sit-com *Absolutely Fabulous*: Clifford, the narrator, is the faultlessly responsible child of an alcohol- and drug-besotted parent mired in the passing fashion of his youth: jazz music. The trumpeter father, Gene, has been subsidized by government largesse his entire adult life and feels no shame about it. What little ingenuity he shows is applied to outfoxing union rules and duping the New York State Bureau of Unemployment. Nor has his wife been any help raising Clifford, and her mental condition raises two related questions: Why do so many children of unstable parents feel compelled to write plays about them? or: Why do children from healthy, nurturing families write so many plays about unstable parents? I'm not convinced there is dramatic gold inherent in this material.

Clifford's narration begins prior to his birth so that he can trace the full disintegration of his parents' relationship. Gene and his future wife, Terry, make love for the first time on a single bed in a dive motel while listening to a bootleg recording of Frank Sinatra. Already we are mired in the trendiness of the jazz milieu, but Leight does manage to create an aura of nostalgia for American life just before fun was made fully electronic.

We are told repeatedly how great Gene and his jazz band are, and other characters are brushed with the stroke of greatness as well: a family friend reflects on Terry's beauty and charisma before she descended into stagy madness: "She was something else back then." But we see Terry and the other adult characters in their youth – can't we judge their appeal ourselves? Doesn't it suggest lack of confidence when a playwright instructs us how to appreciate his flashbacks? The offstage music is interpreted as well: "Genie on a ballad," Clifford informs us, "break[s] your heart every time."

Clifford addresses the audience directly, even mid-scene with other characters present and oblivious. The audience is familiar with this conceit and accepts it; thus, it is jarring late in the second act when Terry inquires of her son, "WHO ARE YOU TALKING TO?" Plus it is no help that the narrator – whom the audience associates closely with the playwright – is a prodigy who skipped two grades by the age of ten. One begins to suspect the unfortunate influence of a dramaturge: irresponsible father, manic-depressive mother, genius son – the elements are all coming together.

Leight must also do battle with the language of his chosen milieu. White musicians named Ziggy and Jonesy talk about "paying dues" and "burning brass" with their "great chops." The material makes this unavoidable, I suppose. But when freed from these constraints, the dialogue still falters. A young Terry reports that the song Gene overheard her playing on her flute was Debussy's "Afternoon of a Faun."

> TERRY: Whatever the fuck a faun is.
> GENE: It's a little deer.
> TERRY: Ohh.
> GENE: ... dear. Useful for crosswords.
> TERRY: (Very impressed) You do crosswords?
> GENE: Sure.
> TERRY: Shit.
> GENE: You know all the four-letter words. I'm surprised you don't know faun.
> TERRY: Screw you ...

Thus a romance is launched. This exchange, I believe, is intended to establish hard-as-nails Terry as a fair match for an experienced jazz musician and his razor-sharp wit. But such wit. It is alarming enough that the dialogue skills of our leading novelists have atrophied over the past decade or so, but when our playwrights fall victim to the same malady, we are in big trouble.

The play comes to a climax when the adult Clifford kicks his father out of the apartment. Terry's mental decline is attributed less to genetic predisposition than to proximity to Gene's carelessness and irresponsibility. In short, Gene is a sad sack who courts failure. Professionally, he cannot or will not see the writing on the wall. When the rise of Elvis Presley and rock 'n' roll signals the end of jazz as a popular genre, Gene is oblivious. And though the new entertainment meccas of Las Vegas and Los Angeles promise steady work to a side man, he sticks stubbornly to his indigent life in New York City. As Clifford tries to explain, "Gene was sort of an anti-psychic." The result is a play with conflict-ridden scenes. But it is a naked contrivance that every path toward a solution is conveniently blocked by Gene's obtuseness. And it is never convincingly explained why Clifford's remarkably talented father, who plays better solos than the visiting featured players, remains a side man, supporting less talented stars and blending in. Is he just unambitious? Add Terry's mental illness, and you get the sense the playwright is piling on, though the drama is reportedly autobiographical. Leight wants to force the narrator to forgo his dream of attending art school and take a lucrative advertising job instead – that is, to sell his soul – in order to pay his parents' bills. For that ultimate sacrifice to be necessary, both parents must be basket cases.

Before the gross amplification of rock 'n' roll guaranteed a sublime musical experience on the cheap, jazz provided a similar rush to those with talent and an aficionado's taste. Thus, Gene dooms himself to a poorly paid career and torments his family just to enjoy the hallucinatory effect of playing his horn. *Side Man* reads like a condemnation of the artist's life when the art form in question is, like jazz, too seductive and narcotic-like. At play's end, Clifford is about to embark on his own artistic career, quitting his job to move west and "make collages." This is both an homage and a rebuke to his father. Like Gene, Clifford ultimately chooses art over a conventional career, but he puts three thousand miles between himself and his old man. And the artistic genre he plans to pursue is a relatively tame one. No one, I believe, ever drove his wife to insanity by obsessively making collages.

Before settling on hot new plays *Bash* and *Betty's Summer Vacation* to complete its *Side Man*-less schedule, Studio Theatre might have considered *Collected Stories*. It has the ingredients of a safe regional theater substitute. The play tells a familiar story, requires only two actors, and is written by an American, Donald Margulies. It also has some funny lines.

The success of staging *Collected Stories* (TCG, 1998) will depend on how the power dynamic between its two characters is played. Ruth, a middle-aged author and university professor, holds a significant advantage from the start over Lisa, a graduate student in her mid-twenties. Lisa acquiesces when Ruth moves their first tutorial from her office to her flat. ("Mainly because I'm a terrible slug.") Ruth offers tea, Lisa requests coffee instead, and Ruth repeats her offer of tea. It is inconsequential to Lisa how she is treated – initially. Studying with the acclaimed writer is "a religious experience" – so much so that she tracks down her idol's uncollected stories in the library so as not to miss a word of scripture. "Is it true you need a new assistant?" Lisa asks, finally getting to the point.

Lisa's tone toward her professor in the first scene suggests a reverential Valley Girl, but with an agenda straight out of *All About Eve*. It is no surprise to the audience when Lisa grows increasingly assertive over the play's six scenes, which cover six years, or that the older woman feels slighted when Lisa's first significant publication comes without the assistance or even foreknowledge of her mentor. This is familiar material from a playwright who teaches playwriting at the Yale School of Drama. (Ruth: "Writing can't be taught.") Like the English-department novel, the writers'-colony novel, and the sabbatical-year-abroad novel, the writing-professor play shows considerable self-consciousness toward its stock characters. As Ruth herself admits, she plays the part of "the feisty older woman who cracks wise and gets away with saying just about anything." These middle-aged ladies – think Allison Lurie or Alice Adams – are an interesting study: assured, single, successful, lonely when they think about it. They command our sympathy at the expense of the Lisa characters – amoral usurpers with rehearsed self-justifications. And every city has its veteran actress for whom this part will be second nature.

Does the over-familiarization of its plot hurt *Collected Stories*? Yes, but not fatally. I've come to the conclusion there are only three kinds of dramatic plots: the contrived plot, the predictable plot, and the nonexistent plot à la Samuel Beckett – my least favorite kind. *Collected Stories* has a predictable plot. But it also has its incidental pleasures and amusing moments, as when Lisa discusses "Eating Between Meals," her short story about a bulimic young woman.

> LISA: Um, the story's kind of autobiographical?
> RUTH: (Feigning surprise) No!
> LISA: I guess that was a stupid thing to say, huh? It's obvious, right?
> RUTH: It's not that it's obvious, it's inconsequential. I don't care what the basis of the story is as long as it's a good story. But did you really stick your finger down your throat like that? I'm joking.

The problem isn't the familiar story arc. Rather, the problem resides in one component of the story and how Margulies handles it. Lisa fashions her professional ascent by using private material from Ruth's life. This results in far too lengthy an exchange of banter written in seminar mode. Ruth: "I think there's something terribly Freudian going on here, don't you?" Lisa: "Oh, come on. You used other people all the time! Don't give me that shit." And, later, Ruth: "You gonna lay some postfeminist crap on me now? Huh, Lisa?"

Margulies, I believe, tries to satirize the bad writing in Lisa's novel, parts of which are read to us: "New York beckoned like a beautiful dark lover with smoky breath and bloodshot eyes." But it's hard to tell because Lisa's prose echoes the overripe dialogue Margulies assigns to Ruth when she recounts her youthful liaison with the poet Delmore Schwartz: "The city was teeming with beatnik poets and old leftists. Smoky bars and late-night sessions. [...] I looked damn good in those tight, coed, Lana Turner sweaters." Near the end of the play, Margulies skillfully weaves a third strand into the plot, explaining the true source of Ruth's envy and anger: her health is beginning to fail. Two of the three plot strands, then, are handled engagingly and poignantly. That's not a bad track record in today's drama.

In some ways, *Collected Stories* resembles Margaret Edson's first play, *Wit* (Faber and Faber, 1999), which enjoyed ecstatic reviews and strong word-of-mouth once it finally made its way to New York City in 1999. The play, according to the author, was turned down by nearly every theater in the country. An elementary school teacher by trade, Edson lacked the professional track record and personal connections to place the script with expedience. For all the credit regional theaters claim for developing new American drama, Edson's experience suggests there is still a limited market even for spectacular work by an unknown. The Studio

Theatre, or any Washington company for that matter, could have scored a coup by staging *Wit* prior to its New York run. Instead, the touring company spent time at the Kennedy Center this year, following *Side Man* by several months.

Wit was first produced at one of the few American theaters that seriously considers submissions by unknown playwrights – South Coast Repertory in Costa Mesa, California – which also commissioned Donald Margulies to write *Collected Stories*. The similarities don't end there. Both plays feature a middle-aged academic confronting her own mortality. Ruth, the emotionally distant writing professor in *Collected Stories* who allows her nurse to call her Mommy, is much like Vivian, the emotionally distant literature professor in *Wit* who allows her nurse to call her sweetheart. Just as Ruth seems to have no family or friends, Vivian is alone for much of her hospitalization. And both parts give veteran actresses the opportunity to commandeer the stage, particularly Vivian, which calls for a shaved head and full frontal nudity.

Vivian Bearing is a fifty-year-old professor of seventeenth-century poetry, specializing in the holy sonnets of John Donne. She addresses the audience directly from the opening line, like Clifford in *Side Man*, guiding us toward the play's inevitable conclusion. ("I think I die in the end.") She prepares the audience and she tries to prepare herself, but it's not easy. "Irony is a literary device that will necessarily be deployed to great effect in this play," she tells us. Her situation is hopeless: she is suffering from stage four metastatic ovarian cancer.

John Donne used wit to confront, stave off, and – his faith assured him – conquer death. ("And death shall be no more, Death thou shalt die.") Why, Vivian asks, can't she do the same? "I thought being extremely smart would take care of it. But I see that I've been found out." Actually, for a good while – the ninety minutes of this play, to be exact – she does succeed in holding death at bay through verbal swordplay. After chemotherapy eradicates her immune system, Vivian reflects.

> I am not in isolation because I have cancer, because I have a tumor the size of a grapefruit. No. I am in isolation because I am being treated for cancer. My treatment imperils my health. Herein lies the paradox. John Donne would revel in it. I would revel in it, if he wrote a poem about it. My students would flounder in it, because paradox is too difficult to understand.

It is tragic that the play's heroine faces her demise before she's truly lived, having devoted her adult life to the meticulous study of a limited cache of short poems. It is at the same time amusing how she deludes herself about the importance of her academic vocation. "I have made an immeasurable contribution to the discipline of English literature," she boasts from her hospital room, where the less learned staff keep busy by saving lives.

If Edson makes one misstep in this brisk, emotionally involving play, it is that she diverts too much attention from the main conflict – Vivian's battle with death – to take swipes at the medical profession. The oncologist who makes Vivian's initial diagnosis is implausibly unfeeling, using technical phrases like "insidious adenocarcinoma" and "primary adnexal mass" that the patient cannot possibly absorb. This gives Vivian the opportunity to parse the diagnosis and analyze it like a poem, the way a literature professor would in a play written by someone who is not a literature professor. Edson worked for a time in a research hospital, and she has clearly boned up on John Donne. But there are times when she is merely parading knowledge.

Much more effective are the simple reflections Vivian offers. "I just hold still and look cancerous," she reports of her medical examinations. "It requires less acting every time." Suffering from a terminal illness, Vivian is an unwitting participant in a drama that has spiraled out of her control. Adding insult to injury, the tone of the script is one she deems unfit for a woman of her intellectual stature and gravity. She laments: "I was dismayed to discover that the play would contain certain ... humorous elements." This, for her, is the ultimate degradation.

It may not be Beckett, but Terrence McNally's *Corpus Christi* (Grove, 1999) is a dramatic work with little or no plot. And though the characters and anecdotes may be familiar, the play is strengthened by that familiarity.

A few seasons ago, the Studio Theatre produced McNally's *Love! Valour! Compassion!*, but Washington theaters were not quick to pounce on *Corpus Christi*. Death threats can do that to a project. As everyone knows, the play concerns a young gay man who is identified as a Christ figure. In September 1998, Catholic groups picketed its premiere at the Manhattan Theater Club. After going momentarily wobbly due to security concerns, the theater stood firm, and McNally was soon exploiting the torture-murder of Matthew Shepard to strengthen his defense of the play. Opportunism on both sides, then, managed to obscure the work, which the published text allows us to consider.

Before it recreates the most familiar episodes from the gospels, the play lingers on the baptism of the disciples, each of whom – either in character or in the voice of the actor playing the character – makes a statement intended to be revealing of something, but I'm not sure what. Thomas: "I'm going to play the shit out of this part." Philip: "I like being Philip." Matthew: "Matthew was a lawyer, a brilliant one. The kind they write novels about." Simon: "I love being Simon."

We subsequently witness the nativity, the performing of miracles, and the crucifixion in the form of a gay bashing. Joshua cures leprosy and blindness, feeds the multitudes, and casts out demons, but he also attends a high school dance in the 1950s in a scene reminiscent of Paula Vogel's *How I Learned to Drive*. This and other nonscriptural episodes have an endearingly amateurish quality and feature lame humor that may owe something to another Vogel work, *The Mineola Twins*.

McNally does not merely update Christ's teachings on love and forgiveness by applying them to the urban homosexual milieu. He also offers his own revelation: "All men are divine." Some of Christianity's traditional censoriousness is retained, though. Joshua declares drugs unnecessary. Philip must be cleansed of his whorish past. And Judas is maligned for insisting penis size matters. As for

Christ's imperative to turn the other cheek, the playwright alternately emphasizes and neglects this commandment as he sees fit.

Is McNally insisting in this play that contemporary gay men are more Christlike than traditional Christians? Or is he merely pointing out the obvious: Christ's core message has relevance for all. McNally's preface to the published text affirms the latter, but at times he does both. He thereby casts his Christ figure in the image of a selfish gay man. When Joshua is informed that his mother wishes to speak to him, he instructs his disciples, "Tell her I have no mother. You are My mother and father and brothers and sisters. You are My family now." The anecdote, I'm afraid, is canonical, but it shows Jesus Christ at his least inspiring. Only by citing scripture very selectively can McNally imply that gay men who neglect their aging parents are Christlike for doing so.

Corpus Christi has weaknesses in spades: the tone shifts abruptly and repeatedly to no good purpose, Judas's motivation is unconvincing (as it is in the gospels), there is numbing repetition, especially in the opening scene. But it should come as no surprise that, ultimately, this material has resonance. Perhaps a monkey could make a compelling drama out of these scenes, but if so, then Terrence McNally is the clever monkey who did. His play about a gay Christ figure may dawdle and sound a bit silly at times, but it remains interesting, and not merely for the ways in which it fails.

Still, news of the London opening of *Corpus Christi* gave me pause. With so many foreign works on Broadway and the regional-theater stages, and with relatively few American plays exported to acclaim, I regretted it was not a more worthy American drama receiving headlines upon its London premiere. But the nature of the publicity was telling: McNally and his play were again receiving threats, this time not from priests but from mullahs. I resist the urge to congratulate someone simply for causing a stir, but I will give McNally credit. He could have chosen to write another contemporary gay comedy like *Love! Valour! Compassion!* or the first act of *The Lisbon Traviata*. Instead he grasped at material that exceeded his reach. How could he know unless he tried?

[2000]

DAVID HARE ON BROADWAY

In November 1997, nearly three years before the most recent eruption of violence in the Middle East, English playwright David Hare returned to London after a brief visit to Israel and wrote a dramatic piece for solo performer: himself. He debuted the work, *Via Dolorosa*, at London's Royal Court Theatre the following September and subsequently performed it for fifteen weeks on Broadway. His diary of the experience, *Acting Up* (Faber and Faber, 1999), chronicles the ordeal of a seasoned playwright pulling double duty as novice stage actor. It commences August 4, 1998, with Hare's first London rehearsal, and ends nearly a year later following the taping of his final two performances in New York City.

Some have questioned if Hare's efforts on stage truly qualify as dramatics. The author quotes Simon Callow's odd note of congratulations: "What you did this evening was a wonderful performance by someone who isn't an actor." Some might further question if the piece is actually a play. *Via Dolorosa*, while fascinating, is not inherently dramatic. The text could best be classified a memoir of Hare's impressions of the Middle East plus a transcript of some of the more politically charged conversations he held there. How – or why – did this essay take shape as a work for the theater? It's a preference, the playwright explains, "what you might call a 'habit of mind' – putting words into other people's mouths." But in this case he puts the words into his own mouth and for an hour and a half pretends to be a theatrical version of himself.

Hare confides that a hundred people must have asked why he chose to take up acting at age fifty-one. "Once I had decided to treat this part of the world," he told them, "there seemed no other honest way to do it. How else could someone from an ignorant, neo-Christian background write clearly about the supreme issues of Jews and Arabs? In this case, you could only trust the witness if you could see who the witness was." Elsewhere, he admits auxiliary motives: "to make me a better director"; "to understand acting better"; "because I had to"; and "to overcome my fear of the audience."

Hare badly underestimates the punishing effort required to perform a ninety-minute monologue eight times a week. He responds to the strain with anger and petulance. By the seventh day of rehearsals, he leaves the theater "white with fury" at his director, Stephen Daldry, from whom he later extorts several sycophantic apologies. Already convinced the entire London theater community wishes his concurrent adaptation, *The Blue Room*, to fail, Hare starts to detect resentment toward his solo project as well. His evidence: friends and colleagues repeatedly insist how brave he is for attempting a one-man show his first time out.

Spleen-venting in diary form is not an unprecedented undertaking for Hare. Included in *Writing Left-Handed* (1991), his collection of short essays, is "The Dead Heart," a sour and paranoid production log of a 1984 staging of *A Map of the World*, directed by the playwright himself. In the introduction to *Writing Left-Handed*, Hare affirms his allegiance to the dramatic form. "I write prose very rarely," he admits. "I have not written consistently for one publication, and a healthy proportion of what I submitted has been rejected by the people who asked for it." The truth is, Hare is an engaging prose stylist as long as one ignores his tendency to enforce double standards. Demands which Hare might consider petty as director or playwright – an actor's request for a telephone and bed in the dressing room, for example – sound reasonable to Hare when made on his own behalf as performer. And I'm convinced any actor who complained as incessantly as the author does about audience coughing would receive an impatient rebuke from David Hare the director.

It may simply be that the veteran playwright cannot help satirizing those around him. It's an old trick: he endears himself to his audience by offering a conspiratorial pact of ill will toward everyone else. There is admittedly something ultimately generous about this diary – generous toward the reader, that is, not toward the author's friends and colleagues who are routinely trashed. As playwright, Hare has never neglected his responsibility to entertain, or divorced himself from the audience for academic, political, or aesthetic reasons. As diarist, he shoulders his responsibilities in much the same way.

For example, in his October 1, 1998, diary entry, he writes:

> Luca Barbareschi, the director and star of the Italian production of [Hare's play] *Skylight*, was waiting for me when I got to the theatre. With him was the actress Lucrezia Lante Della Rovere, who plays Kyra. They had previously acted together in David Mamet's *Oleanna*. This has been true all over the world: the actors who create *Skylight* have often done *Oleanna*. They said *Oleanna* made no sense in Italy because the concept of political correctness does not exist there. The actress said, 'You see, I like having my bottom pinched. It makes me feel men desire me, and I like that feeling.' I asked how it went. 'Well,' said Luca, 'when it got to the bit where I hit her, they all stood up and shouted "Kill the bitch."'

At first, the author is apprehensive about the subject matter of *Via Dolorosa*, and hesitant to perform the play in the United States because of the inflammatory political content. "American Jews would resent my speaking about the Middle East," he speculates in the middle of his London run, "and there would surely be a distracting row." Hare's fears are assuaged when his London performances incite no heckling but, rather, elicit comments from scholars and Middle Easterners assuring him of the text's validity. The New York reception is, if anything, more serious and respectful, despite the fact that Hare includes the following passages: (1) Assured by novelist Philip Roth that the Jewish settlers are absolute lunatics – "the maddest people I've ever met in my life" – Hare has an involuntary thought en route to a settlement: *the Jews do not belong here*. (2) The author's hosts suspect Prime Minister Yitzhak Rabin collaborated on his own assassination merely to make life more difficult for the settlers. (3) Shulamit Aloni, a former official in the Rabin government, grows impatient with Hare's confusion about the political stalemate. "What's so difficult to understand?" she demands. "The Jews were once victims, so now we are brainwashed to believe we will always be victims and victims can do no wrong." And (4) the Palestinians, for their part, seem secretly pleased by perennial diplomatic and economic failure. They have found meaning in their crisis-filled lives and fear progress might bring disillusionment.

"It's like *Plenty*," Hare's British Council handler tells him, referring to one of the author's most successful plays, from 1978, in which the main character – a participant in the resistance movement in France – returns to London at the end of World War II. Having witnessed acts of true bravery and kindness by people of absolute conviction, she finds herself a misfit back home, impatient with the peacetime English who, unchallenged and unbelieving, seem "childish and a little silly."

Faith, Hare realizes, has been his subject as playwright for some time. It is featured explicitly in *Racing Demon* (1990), the dual story of a faithless vicar who views his mission as social work and an evangelical colleague keen on filling the pews by emphasizing the supernatural. It is arguable which of the two better serves his parishioners: the one who feeds useful illusion, or the one who offers levelheaded doubt. A similar ambivalence permeates *Via Dolorosa*. The Jewish settlers and the Palestinian refugees are fanatical in their adherence to self-defeating tactics and beliefs, but draw comfort on some deeper level from their futile persistence. By contrast, "[M]aterialism has so sapped Western man that he has reached some sort of dispirited state at which he no longer believes that the best of his dreams and wishes can be embodied in his social ideals." So laments Hare in "When Shall We Live?," the Eric Symes Abbot Memorial Lecture paired by his publishers in a single volume with *Via Dolorosa* (Faber and Faber, 1998). The result in England is a Labour Party that cannot use the word "socialism," and an Anglican Church that dares not mutter the name "Christ."

Hare's Jewish-settlement hosts stop backstage after a New York performance to vent their fury. The playwright made them appear foolish in his monologue, they complain. But in truth Hare has a deep reservoir of sympathy for these absolute lunatics and their settler neighbors, many of whom were raised in the United States but who tired of America as a place where life is materialistic and empty. "My whole life, I've been told: 'Western civilization? An old bitch gone in the teeth,'" Hare explains at the very beginning of his monologue. "And so people say, go to Israel. Because in Israel at least people are fighting. In Israel, they're fighting for something they believe in." So Hare went to Israel. The result is a work about a person of no faith encountering people with nothing but faith.

"People thirst for this kind of recognition of real life," Hare writes in his diary, referring to the eagerness of audiences to embrace an unconventional play about important political matters. *Via Dolorosa* became a word-of-mouth hit in New York in spring 1999, closing to packed houses after 113 performances. "Yet we go on offering Noël fucking Coward and domestic gagfests," the author laments. "It makes me furious."

[2001]

A British Mini-Boom

The British playwright David Edgar charts the path of British theater over the past decade in his introduction to *State of Play: Playwrights on Playwriting* (Faber and Faber, 1999), but he does a great deal more than that. In thirty-two pages the author of *Pentecost*, *Destiny*, and the Royal Shakespeare Company's *Nicholas Nickleby* adaptation canvasses more than four hundred years of British dramatic history, emphasizing in particular three epochs dominated by new writing: the Elizabethan-Jacobean period, the Restoration, and the years between 1890 and 1914, which boasted the great works of Oscar Wilde and George Bernard Shaw. Each era of vibrant new drama occurred in the wake of a major upheaval, Edgar observes. The defeat of the Spanish Armada, the overthrow of the Puritan commonwealth, and the triumph of industrial capitalism each produced an audience "hungry to come to terms with the consequent social and cultural change."

Edgar means to place in context a fourth boom in playwriting – or miniboom – spanning the past decade. "Once again, it seems, theatre has found a subject at the heart of the zeitgeist," he remarks. This newest renaissance in playwriting is the culmination of several bursts of creativity following the Second World War, which gave rise to the works of John Osborne and other Angry Young Men of the 1950s. Feminist authors launched playwriting careers throughout subsequent decades, just as British women outside the world of theater were closing the gap in work-force participation and redefining their roles vis-à-vis men. That, Edgar suggests, led to the cataclysm that generated the major theme of 1990s playwrights – the crisis of masculinity.

"They were once again plays about the unintended consequences of huge social changes," Edgar notes of these new works, "plays which appear about twenty years after great tectonic shifts in the political, cultural and economic geology of the times. The decline of the dominant role of men – in the workplace and in the family – is probably the biggest single story of the last thirty years in the western countries, and it has given a whole new generation of young male playwrights – and some women playwrights too – a subject to embrace."

Twenty-five theater colleagues contribute to *State of Play*, an assemblage of oral reports culled from ten years of annual drama conferences held at the University of Birmingham, where Edgar teaches. Some contributors sound unconvinced that the recent trend toward male-centered drama constitutes a renaissance in playwriting, but none directly refutes the trend's existence. Tim Firth's *Neville's Island*, Jez Butterworth's *Mojo*, Simon Bent's *Goldhawk Rd*, Terry Johnson's *Dead Funny*, and Kevin Elyot's *My Night with Reg* are among the titles Edgar cites. Athletics and gambling – guy stuff – often feature in the stories, and many works are set in a vague criminal underworld of violent sexual practices, drug use, and petulant irresponsibility. Some authors parade the banality of their material in titles like *Shopping and Fucking*. Nihilism rules.

The British drama critic Benedict Nightingale is quoted throughout *States of Play*, primarily because he detected the masculinity-in-crisis trend early and observed that these new dramatists, unlike their predecessors, have "no obvious ideology, no political credo, no social agenda." Such is the intellectual landscape of the post-Thatcher boom in British drama, and not everyone is pleased by it. The playwright Rebecca Prichard resents how plays showcasing masculinity, youth, and nihilism silence the playwright as social critic. "We end up with plays which are a strange celebration of masculine culture but which at the same time totally emasculate theatre. They are supposed to look at power but they trivialize it."

In contrast, William Gaminara welcomes the proliferation of plays dealing with "genuine contemporary masculine problems." Such works would never have received a hearing in the 1980s, he claims, because of the exclusive emphasis at that time on the experience of women. And he charges feminist authors with inconsistency. "After all," he notes, "it's hard to criticize men for delving into their emotional lives if you've been repeatedly accusing them of not being able to do precisely that." British women were now getting heavy doses of men's emotional lives and realizing they may not want access after all.

In his introduction, Edgar diagrams the perennial three-way conversation in Britain over the purpose of art: one voice speaks for the patrician model, which sees art's role as ennobling the citizens of the nation; a second voice speaks for the popular model, for which art's primary purpose is to entertain consumers; and a third voice speaks for the provocative model, which defines the role of the arts as challenging the community's complacency. An instructive contrast can be drawn to the same conversation over the purpose of art in America, which lacks a longstanding elite cultural tradition of its own and, thus, features a weak, borrowed patrician model, a super-strong popular model, and an ersatz provocative model that commands the loyalty of complacent, middle-thinking playwrights. Edgar further examines the Blaire government's cultural policies, presents statistical analyses of London theater attendance, notes the absence of the filmed play from the BBC, and considers the effects of television and cinema – particularly of bleak and violent Hollywood films – on playwriting. What Edgar fails to do, however, is fully credit the Soviet Union's implosion and the triumph of Thatcherism for the vogue of anti-ideological writing – a connection made more explicit by other participants.

"[It] goes back to 1989 – as so many things in the 1990s do – when a sudden hole was blasted in the middle of so many people's central beliefs, and there was a collective feeling of having the rug pulled from people's feet," declares Gaminara about the recent crop of nonideological, men-only plays. David Greig observes, "There is a sense that ideology itself is embarrassing, that no one believes that things can ever change or ought ever to be changed in the political culture." A running theme in Greig's work, offered instead of nihilistic violence, is a fascination with characters who stubbornly believe in things – "socialism, communism or Christianity" – which they know to be untrue.

The Thatcher years were a period of significant upheaval, with free market ideas surviving the demise of utopian socialism. What sort of writing emerges from that? Based on Edgar's historical model, we should be witnessing a mob of Tory sympathizers thriving in the arts, invigorated by the triumph of the marketplace and its proven efficiencies. But with the obvious exception of Tom Stoppard, today's classical liberals, it seems, do not write plays. If they did, they would sound detached and uninspiring, at least compared to predecessors who offered earnest pleas for egalitarianism and economic justice. Those who denigrated the nanny state for its nationalized industries and its public-welfare programs are nowhere to be seen on the London stage; instead the defeated retain control. It's as if dethroned Puritans somehow managed to dominate Restoration drama; or, in lieu of Shakespeare, Marlowe, and Kyd, a group of Spanish sailors washed up on shore and inaugurated the literary Renaissance in Elizabethan England. For forty years, committed leftists in Britain faulted the postwar Labour government of Clement Attlee for its halfhearted attempts to implement a truly emancipatory socialism. The same people today acknowledge this was no lost opportunity after all – a feasible chance at emancipation never existed. As a result, the theatrical landscape has changed significantly in Britain. We now have dramatic writing that eschews a sincere political stance and assumes all fundamental beliefs are necessarily false. In short, we have nihilism, testosterone, and insincere consumerism. We have shopping and fucking. We have pulp fiction.

Like *State of Play*, Alex Sierz's *In-Yer-Face Theatre* (Faber and Faber, 2001) considers the resurgence of playwriting in 1990s Britain. The books are not precisely redundant, though: Edgar examines the *male* in the young-male-playwright equation, while Sierz focuses on the *young* and examines the works of a number of women playwrights as well. The authors Sierz finds most compelling constitute a small group of provocative antagonists who smash taboos, mention the forbidden, and create discomfort. Their language is fast, sharp, direct – and generally filthy; their characters "talk about unmentionable subjects, take their clothes off, have sex, humiliate [one] another, experience unpleasant emotions, become suddenly violent." Sierz finds these works "thrillingly alive" and "experiential."

The book offers as a representative work of in-yer-face drama the following synopsis of a play written by twenty-one-year-old Peter Rose. "*Snatch* begins with two students, Paul and Simon, boasting about a girl they've picked up and raped during the night. As dawn breaks, a huddled figure lying on the back of the stage begins to move. When she gets up, Beth is trembling and covered in bruises." Simon exits, and Paul assaults Beth again. "Suddenly, there is a red flash and Beth and Paul swap bodies. Now Beth strides around the room showing off 'her' muscles and Paul cowers, defenseless in a woman's body. Beth gags and ties him up. When Simon returns, she invites him to abuse 'Beth,' and he does so, unaware that he is having sex with his mate. Beth returns with a tattoo on 'her' forehead. It reads RAPIST. Simon is appalled. Then Beth cuts off 'her' penis. As the blood spreads, there is another flash and Beth and Paul swap bodies again. Beth blinds Simon and leaves, shouting, 'I'll get over this – I will.'"

Though I harbor a soft spot for vigilante justice, I found this synopsis ludicrous. Sierz credits in-yer-face authors with putting an ossified British theater establishment back in touch with youth culture. But what connection is there between today's youth and the world depicted in *Snatch*? (Saffron Monsoon, the uptight daughter on *Absolutely Fabulous*, seems as typical of the younger generation as do these brazen tag-team rapists.) I reacted to the play synopsis with profound sorrow and anger, not at the playwright, but at a feminist establishment that has managed to warp the mind of a young man into producing such self-emasculating work. The rape impulse does derive from masculinity, of course, but so does the impulse to impose an ethical system of order on those who would commit rape, which is why the impunity with which Rose's representative characters pursue their gleeful criminality makes no sense outside a world shaped by feminist hysteria.

Unfortunately, other plays the author cites sound equally misguided. In addition to *Snatch*, Sierz examines the oeuvres of Mark Ravenhill, Anthony Neilson, and the late Sarah Kane, and he considers single works by other writers, including Patrick Marber's *Closer*, *The War Boys* by American Naomi Wallace, and the stage version of Irvine Welsh's novel *Trainspotting*. Mamet, Pinter, and Beckett are mentioned most often as influences on the group, though Ravenhill cites moralistic 1980s American Brat-Pack novels (*Less Than Zero*, *Bright Lights, Big City*) as personal influences as well. It is no surprise, then, that Ravenhill finds the chic French theorists of violence – Foucault, Baudrillard – irresponsible and reactionary. Still, "irresponsible" is a word hostile critics use to describe the works of Ravenhill and other young playwrights.

And indeed, in a local sense, their productions do neglect basic safety concerns. Sierz attended Neilson's kinetic, knife-riddled play *Penetrator* in a tiny attic theater. "[I]ts ninety minutes with no break were relentlessly frightening," he reports, "because of the acute sense of imminent danger and the real possibility of actors injuring themselves or one of the spectators."

This raises a fundamental point. When there is the threat of actual knife wounds or severe bruising in a theater space, or when toilet functions are performed on stage, the effect may be visceral and shocking, but audience members find themselves silently questioning the judgment of the playwright or objecting to demands imposed on the actors. They stop believing in the characters, in other words, and the experience thereafter ceases to be theater and becomes instead an unpleasant form of living, confined artificially to a stage. The fictive dream is interrupted, as it is in cinema when a Hollywood actor puts on a lot of weight for a role: at the end of *Raging Bull*, we watch a fat actor named Robert DeNiro reciting dialogue – his character, Jake LeMotta, has left the movie.

The same thing happens when sex is detailed explicitly: the characters are forgotten. For Sierz, nude scenes raise questions about privacy and voyeurism; actually showing sex, he feels, unsettles audience members because "it is a reminder of many of our most intimate feelings, and of what we most desire to keep secret." But it is also a reminder that, if the actress is short of rent money this month, stage nudity and simulated sex amount to thespian prostitution. Again, in such an environment our attention is drawn away from the character to the actor.

Even in a novel, sex scenes are to be dreaded because readers may sense the author considers his fantasies or sexual experiences more erotically charged than theirs and believes the intensity of his and his partner's orgasms warrants fictionalized scrutiny. What makes these passages so uncomfortable is not our prudishness but, rather, the near certainty with which we face authorial self-delusion.

The same could be said of in-yer-face drama as a whole. Like overwrought acting, confrontational playwriting can easily fail to elicit its intended response – shock, say, or revulsion – and instead evoke mirthful derision. I certainly found Sierz's capsule summaries unintentionally amusing. "Helplessly blind, Ian masturbates, defecates, and eats the baby," is how he sums up a scene from Sarah Kane's *Blasted*. During a performance of Ravenhill's *Shopping and Fucking*, he recounts, "the sight of Mark rising with his mouth bloody from rimming Gary provoked groans."

It was a pleasant surprise, then, to read passages culled directly from interviews with the playwrights. With interference from Sierz reduced to a minimum, the subjects acquit themselves nicely. Anthony Neilson, for example, suggests that a play should invigorate an audience the way a rock 'n' roll band does. He therefore attempts in his work to produce an emotional rather than intellectual reaction. This precludes setting out to write a play with a conscious political agenda. "Tell a story," he instructs, "and the themes will take care of themselves." Mark Ravenhill's philosophy is more pithy: "Don't be boring." But how do we get from this to gouged eyeballs, cannibalism, and the castrating feminist agitprop of Peter Rose's *Snatch*? "Usually, when writers use shock tactics, it is because they have something urgent to say," Sierz asserts. But I get the distinct impression shock tactics serve primarily as a short cut to notoriety, which would explain a lot.

[2002]

Tom Stoppard, American

In 1998, the prestigious Comédie-Française theater in Paris added to its repertoire Tom Stoppard's masterpiece *Arcadia*. It was the first time a play by a living foreign writer had received this honor. In his introduction to *Arcadia's* published French edition, translator Jean-Marie Besset wryly observed "this is, so to speak, an almost French play" – meaning a play acclaimed and institutionalized in France, written by a British author of Czech origin.

I approached *Tom Stoppard: A Life*, Ira Nadel's new biography, intending quite similarly to claim the playwright as an almost American author. From Nadel's account, there is much in Stoppard's history to support such a claim, at least superficially. As a youngster, Tomáš Sträussler was educated at an American-run boarding school in Darjeeling, India, where he learned English with an American accent, which he later lost. He also took to playing baseball prior to assuming a lifelong passion for cricket. After relocating to England – and taking his stepfather's family name – Stoppard found British literature slightly quaint, whereas American writing, particularly the short stories of Ernest Hemingway, was infused for him with excitement and glamour. And the playwright's triumphant arrival in New York in the 1960s elicited affection from the American public that matched his own for the United States. As Nadel explains, Stoppard was the intellectuals' answer to the British invasion in popular music, with *Rosencrantz and Guildenstern Are Dead* (1966), his first major play, serving as his *Meet the Beatles*. Stoppard, with his rubbery lips, lank frame, and untutored hair, even bore a resemblance to another invading Briton, Mick Jagger.

But the Beatles and the Rolling Stones were not American bands, after all, and Stoppard is just as clearly English. In fact, Nadel makes much of the fact that Stoppard, with his extensive collections of English watercolors and first-edition books by English authors, was pressured to assimilate, or hyper-assimilate, by both his immigrant Czech mother and his English stepfather. "Stoppard more than once noted that his mother feared that British chauvinism would put him and his brother at a disadvantage among his new peers if much was made of their foreignness," Nadel writes. "Consequently, just as she hid or denied their Jewish past, they, in turn, took to England and English boarding-school life with enthusiasm and energy manifesting itself in their drive to be as English as possible." Though Nadel attempts to analyze the adult Stoppard within this same context, the playwright himself rejects the thesis as the key to a true understanding of his life, his mind, or his dramatic works.

Stoppard's intellectual calm serves as queer antidote to a tension-filled life, which includes a flight from Nazism (all four grandparents perished in the Holocaust); a close escape from the Japanese occupation of Singapore, which his father died fleeing; relocation to India; and, finally, resettlement in England and a life of acting British and politely ignoring the possibility of his own Jewish ancestry. Even startling midlife revelations about his family's heritage and long-delayed reports of his mother's Czech siblings surviving the war leave Stoppard unrattled, though reflective. "I was vaguely pleased when I found out," Stoppard allows. "But it's too late to pretend that somehow you're different because you've learned something."

Stoppard concedes that he's had quite an interesting life "by some standards," but even a life this eventful does not guarantee a compelling biography. In his introduction, Nadel quotes a passage from one of Virginia Woolf's diaries: "let the biographer present fully, completely, accurately, the known facts without comment; then let him write the life as fiction." Nadel, a professor of English at the University of British Columbia, shovels the facts but neglects the fiction, by which I mean a driving narrative that can propel the book and make sense of the details, which at times overwhelm the project.

For example, I was interested in the biographer's account of several months the aspiring playwright spent in Berlin in 1964 on a Ford Foundation grant, not least because Stoppard, having seen Peter Weiss's *Marat/Sade* upon its German premiere, used a similar play-within-a-play technique in subsequent works, including *The Real Thing*. But was it necessary for the biographer to catalogue the other Ford fellows residing in Berlin, and to report that one of them, the American Tom Cullinan (who seems to have had no influence on Stoppard's work and little impact on his life), two years later published a novel (*The Beguiled*) about a wounded soldier in the U.S. Civil War, and that in the 1971 film version of the story the soldier was played by Clint Eastwood? Not only do we read about Stoppard's professional relationships with Kenneth Tynan and Laurence Olivier, we are also offered a several-paragraph explication of Tynan and Olivier's rocky relationship, which again carries no clear implications for Stoppard's career.

Near the end of the book, in the acknowledgments, Nadel belatedly fills us in: "Tom Stoppard has been from the first a skeptical but supportive witness to the entire project." It sounds like Nadel never benefited from Stoppard's direct input. Citing extant interviews and essays, Nadel still offers some interesting observations about Stoppard's writing. For example, since his early days as a journalist, the playwright has been willing to revise his works to serve the needs of the moment; in theater, this manifests itself in a readiness to shift, cut, or otherwise modify the text to fit a production, because for Stoppard – as Nadel tells us a dozen or more times – a play is a malleable event, not a fixed script on the page. Stoppard also derives satisfaction from writing adaptations, translations, and screenplays based on novels (*Empire of the Sun*, *The Russia House*) because, he says, the work is easy. "I find it difficult to invent a story situation and people," he admits. Thus, he works frequently as a script doctor in Hollywood. (He won an Oscar for his contributions to *Shakespeare in Love* and received a million-dollar "thank-you bonus" from Steven Spielberg for his work on one of the Indiana Jones movies.) Stoppard's aversion to plot-and-character invention has implications for his own plays, which sometimes riff on famous dramatic works (*Hamlet* and *The Importance of Being Earnest*) or, as in *Arcadia*, pinch their plots from narratives in other media – in that case, A.S. Byatt's novel *Possession*.

As I said, this is interesting material, but I've encountered much of it previously in Mel Gussow's *Conversations with Stoppard* and the similarly titled *Tom Stoppard in Conversation*, edited by Paul Dellany. Since Nadel is dependent on secondary sources, the biographer might have focused his analysis on Stoppard's status as a political conservative thriving in the anglophone theater world, since this is a subject Stoppard is repeatedly asked to comment on in interviews. "Conservative playwright," of course, is an oxymoronic phrase in the American dialect. How is Britain so different that a Czech immigrant can chart a brilliant career as a dramatist while expressing admiration for Margaret Thatcher and mocking self-adulatory political activists on the left? Such mockery in *The Real Thing*, Nadel notes, led to complaints in 1982 – "from David Hare most forcibly" – that Stoppard had come out of the closet of apologetic conservatism and surrendered his "good-natured neutrality." But in 1995, Mel Gussow quoted David Hare to support the contention that Stoppard's liberal peers have great respect for his integrity. "I never find him politically narrow," Hare avowed. "We have more in common than in conflict."

What happened in the intervening twelve years? Or was the quote outdated? Tracing the reception of Stoppard's political views might have provided the "fiction" this biography needs and might have permitted the reader to hold Stoppard up, not as an honorary American, but as the prototype for a new breed of American playwright that could broaden and invigorate the political dialogue on our stages – or, rather, finally initiate a dialogue.

[2003]

Political Stages

On the night of October 6, 1998, Russell Henderson and Aaron McKinney chatted in a Laramie, Wyoming, bar with a university student named Matthew Shepard. Offered a ride in their truck, Shepard accepted. Soon after departing, however, the townies turned violent, pistol whipping their passenger before dumping him, barely breathing, beside a running path on the outskirts of the city. The next day a bicyclist came upon the apparently lifeless form and called for help. At the Laramie hospital, a physician attending to McKinney for unrelated injuries asked his patient to wait while he attempted in vain to treat the new arrival, who subsequently died from blows inflicted by McKinney the previous night.

So went the horrific events that ignited an explosion of media coverage culminating a year later in the sentencing of the murderers. Moisés Kaufman's theater piece *The Laramie Project* (Vintage, 2001) both acknowledges and contributes to that explosion. ("It was huge," Kaufman quotes Jon Peacock, Shepard's academic advisor, describing the inundation of Laramie, population 26,687. "[W]e're talking hundreds of reporters.") The author and nine members of his Tectonic Theater Project traveled from New York City to Wyoming on six separate occasions, beginning one month after the attack, to speak with more than 200 townspeople. They transcribed, ordered, and honed the interviews into this collaborative "project," which they performed at its New York premiere. The play has subsequently been produced professionally in most major U.S. cities and staged by university theater departments across the country.

As early as 1986, playwright Maria Irene Fornes bemoaned the direction in which politically engaged playwrights such as Emily Mann and Adrian Hall – Kaufman's predecessors – were heading: toward a journalistic style of writing. "Some people are doing actual documentaries," she complained, predicting that such pieces had no staying power. "That's not theater literature," she griped. "It may be serious and subtle work but it's not a play." Having recently reread *Execution of Justice*, Mann's theater documentary from the mid-1980s about the double assassination of San Francisco Mayor George Moscone and Supervisor Harvey Milk, I can discount Fornes's prediction: such works, when skillfully assembled, retain considerable power as literature, as plays. It bodes well, then, that Kaufman and his team of collaborators bring significant skill to *The Laramie Project*. But they face an obstacle that Mann, twenty years ago, did not face, and which Fornes could not have anticipated: the interference of self-consciousness on the part of the interviewees who, far from refusing to cooperate, begin to play along. At a time when television shows are scripted, massaged, and edited to appear spontaneous, nonprofessional participants have caught on to the efficacy of acting out, which increases the storyline's drama, the series' ratings, and the participant's own share of screen time. I'm not the first to make this or similar observations. Playwrights Spalding Gray and Anna Deavere Smith have cited the obstacles they now face encountering the great mass of amateur performers. And Mark Steyn in his review of *The Laramie Project* reported that residents of Oklahoma City, having been asked repeatedly by television journalists if their community needed time to heal after the Timothy McVeigh bombing, began to volunteer that information with a minimum of prompting, using the precise wording sought by the journalists. He cited a similar example of inauthentic dialogue from the script of *The Laramie Project*. "We don't grow children like that here," one townsperson, referring to the murderers, wistfully asserts before conceding, "Well, it's pretty clear that we do grow children like that here."

I would offer in turn a quote by Harry Woods, a gay resident of Laramie immobilized by a leg cast the day of the University of Wyoming's homecoming parade. Woods describes how a banner commemorating Matthew Shepard passed by one side of his apartment, trailed by a crowd of a hundred or so supporters, and later passed by the other side, followed by five times that number. "And people kept joining in," Woods tells a member of the theater company. "And you know what? I started to cry. Tears were streaming down my face. And I thought, 'Thank God that I got to see this in my lifetime.' And my second thought was, 'Thank you, Matthew.'"

Were those his actual thoughts? Did his mind actually form the sentence, *Thank you, Matthew*? If so, the insidious effects of reality television and infotainment are worse than suspected: viewers no longer merely report their experiences in the language required of them by media celebrities; they have actually begun to experience their lives through that language.

As testament to the inherent strength and journalistic immediacy of this form of drama, though, most of the collected interview excerpts, whether spontaneous or coached, are compelling. Doc O'Connor, a local entrepreneur, offers a mathematical take on the local society of homosexual men: "There's more gay people in Wyoming than meets the eye," he reasons. "If there's eight men and one woman in a Wyoming bar, which is often the case, now you stop and think – who's getting what? You see what I'm saying?" Marge Murray, a retired bartender, condones the *laissez faire* attitude of most Laramie residents toward homosexuals. "I don't give a damn one way or the other as long as they don't bother me," she states. "And even if they did, I'd just say no thank you. And that's the attitude of most of the Laramie population." Still, other anecdotal reflections suggest the environment is not so easygoing. A theater student at the university recalls that his parents made no objection when he played a murderer in *Macbeth*, but balked when he auditioned for the role of Prior in *Angels in America*, because "homosexuality is a sin." An openly lesbian faculty member finds herself a social pariah, not among her straight colleagues, but among closeted lesbians who fear the public stain of association. And Jonas Slonaker dismisses Laramie's tolerant reputation out of hand, claiming it simply boils down to: "If I don't tell you I'm a fag, you won't beat the crap out of me. I mean, what's so great about that? That's a great philosophy?"

Kaufman and his collaborators order this material effectively, presenting the robbery-murder in the context of class differences. "It's about the well-educated and the ones that are not," notes Murray. Matt Galloway, the bartender who served Shepard his last drink, draws the clearest distinctions. Matthew Shepard was the perfect customer, in his estimation. He possessed an appealing triumvirate of manners, politeness, and intelligence. McKinney and Henderson, by way of contrast, lacked proper social skills. His assessment of them: "Dirty. Grungy. Rude." "Money meant nothing to Matthew," Shepard's townie friend Romaine Patterson adds, "because he came from a lot of it."

Some of those interviewed are permitted to make accusations of unfairness and exploitation against the media and – by implication at least – against members of the Tectonic Theater Project. "Had this been a heterosexual these two boys decided to take out and rob, this never would have made the national news," states Bill McKinney, father of Aaron. "Now my son is guilty before he's even had a trial." This, it seems to me, is a point in need of substantial development, which the author is unable to provide because he and his collaborators interviewed only locals when a broader historical perspective was required. Throughout the past century when anarchists, Stalinists, or other radicals were involved in high-profile legal cases, political activists and artists routinely insisted that the culpability of the accused was immaterial when it could be argued that they had been subjected to politically tainted prosecution and thereby denied a fair trial. (I am thinking specifically of Sacco and Vanzetti, the Rosenbergs, and Mumia Abu-Jamal.) But in this case, the apparent guilt of two politically odious twenty-one year olds quelled the need for a fair trial. In fact, their choice of victim – a waifish gay man – was widely seen as justifying the conscription of additional law-enforcement personnel and other exceptional resources, provided under the auspices of hate-crime legislation, to facilitate a guilty verdict. The reason for this inconsistency is fairly obvious: McKinney and Henderson's acts could not be twisted into serving a political cause popular among the press and intelligentsia, but their victim's suffering could. One might not weep for the demonstrably guilty when they are condemned under suspect circumstances, but one should nevertheless be alarmed by overt manipulation of the legal system, which *The Laramie Project* tacitly condones.

A much more fundamental weakness of the play is the inaccessible central character, whose personality has been gutted of complexity in the name of inert hagiography – a genre Kaufman resurrects from medieval drama. "Out of the Shepard tragedy is wrenched art," promises a blurb from the *New York Post*, hinting at an element in the source material – the protagonist's fatal flaw – that the author simply will not acknowledge, and will not permit others to acknowledge. Like the depressing tale of a drunken coed who is raped while unconscious, Shepard's story – which in no way exonerates the murderers – is, in dramatic terms, more a tragedy than the melodrama of victimization Kaufman constructs, and it provides a survival lesson: the first order of the day must always be self-preservation. We are never informed here that defense lawyers collected evidence about Matthew Shepard's history of sexually accosting straight male friends, whose gut response to his intrusive gestures was to strike him. The persistent threat of violent retribution seems to have heightened the thrill of possible sexual conquest for the real Matthew Shepard – but not for Kaufman's absent protagonist of the same name. One can challenge the admissibility of such evidence as part of a "gay panic" defense in a trial, but *The Laramie Project* is a work for the theater, not a legal proceeding; the witnesses are contributing to a narrative quilt, not sitting for a deposition. It is an egregious oversight on the part of the troupe's interviewers that they did not elicit information from friendly sources about Matthew Shepard's inner demons; it is a graver dramaturgical sin if they suppressed that information. In the theater, rounded characters – even those kept offstage – are primarily the sum of their inner demons, particularly those that lead to their tragic demise.

"When the 'don't ask, don't tell' policy came into effect in 1993, a group of military personnel was silenced by law," writes Kaufman in his introduction to Marc Wolf's *Another American: Asking and Telling*, included in *Political Stages*, a new anthology edited by Emily Mann and David Roessel (Applause, 2002). "But by conducting interviews and writing this play," Kaufman continues, "Marc has given these men and women a voice."

In the tradition of Mann and Kaufman, Wolf transcribed taped interviews with an assortment of Americans – "straight, gay, and lesbian military personnel, veterans from WWII to Desert Storm, civil rights lawyers, federal judges, politicians, activists, and professors of sociology, constitutional law and military history" – and assembled monologues that appear on the page like stuttering, disjointed poetry, providing snapshots of honorable persons embroiled in a surprisingly intractable dilemma. Also like Mann, whose most famous play considers the political fault lines between gay and straight constituents in San Francisco, and Kaufman, who prior to taking on *The Laramie Project* rose to prominence with *Gross Indecency: The Three Trials of Oscar Wilde*, Wolf considers a political maelstrom framed by society's official discomfort with homosexuality. This should come as no surprise. Not only is homosexuality a naggingly persistent source of contention in a nation long conversant on the subject, but the theater world – centered in urban areas, particularly New York City – plays to an audience inordinately comprising gay men. Even the aforementioned Mark Steyn, as drama critic for the neoconservative *New Criterion*, has conceded the reality of what he calls "the core gayness of the theater."

"Any actor in America can pick up the play, and with very little else, perform it," Kaufman asserts of Wolf's one-man show. "It doesn't need extensive sets or costumes." Yet the play's website (www.anotheramerican.com) suggests that only Wolf has been permitted to stage the work thus far, at a dozen first-rate theaters including the Mark Taper Forum in Los Angeles and the New Group in New York. Wolf has wisely exerted control over nearly every aspect of the play's production and composition. It is especially important that Wolf conducted the interviews himself, since he is sensitive to and knowledgeable about American life west of the Hudson River, unlike some members of the Tectonic Theater Project who expected to be accosted by homophobic outlaws on the streets of small-town Wyoming. ("I was really frightened driving into Laramie at dusk," Leigh Fondakowski, Moisés Kaufman's head writer, admitted to *American Theatre* magazine. "It took me four trips to feel safe jogging there.")

"I knew it would be important to find people who could persuasively argue the military's point of view," Wolf writes in his foreword. Among the most effective voices is that of a retired Army Colonel; as a squad leader training enlisted men for Vietnam, he became aware that one of his recruits, named Gotta, was "blowing everybody in the squad" and suffering retribution for his sexual compliance. "These guys got it on with Gotta, then felt guilty about it, got a few beers in them, and used him as a human punching bag," the Colonel explains. This weakened unit cohesion, naturally, and the solution seemed simple: get rid of Gotta. "Then my squad got together, and they became very effective."

A no-nonsense counter-argument is made by Bridget Wilson, an activist lawyer formerly enlisted in the U.S. Army, who notes the folly of an organization that for a long time expelled female employees who got married or pregnant. "And then they're sitting around going 'Where'd all these dykes come from?'"

Falling not exactly in between but to the side in this debate is an anonymous young enlisted soldier disgusted at the media's obsession with something as peripheral as the official status of gay servicemen when his unit, which could be deployed at moment's notice, lacks cold weather jackets, standard boots, and live ammunition for target practice. If the government were to drop the "don't ask, don't tell" policy and admit openly gay servicemen, he observes, it would "start a firestorm of debate" that more pressing concerns could never generate. A democratic society with a free press, he implies, gets the quality of military it deserves.

Like Kaufman, Wolf sometimes elicits stagy language from his interview subjects. A former U.S. Marine Corps Corporal named Ed Clayton provides three separate monologues that, even if true, sound fabricated. In the first, he recounts a sexual experience with a drill instructor at boot camp that could have been cribbed from any number of pornographic movies, and which comes complete with a funny tag line: "I don't want people to get the idea that the marine corps is rampant with homosexual activity but it is." Things get more implausible and conveniently literary in his two subsequent monologues. It was a mistake for Wolf to include them.

More cogently, Miriam Ben Shalom, a former Staff Sergeant in the Army Reserve, tries to nail the lid shut on what for all appearances is a simple case.

> I mean we aren't talking about sashaying down the main drag of the military base
>   while wearing lavender fatigues,
>   we aren't talking about misbehaving you know
>   or bad conduct here.
> We're talking about speech.

But what about bad conduct? What about sashaying down the main drag? At a time when "queer" behavior has been defined, by self-appointed queer spokesmen, as relentlessly combative – as behavior disruptive of the status quo – doesn't the military have something to fear from open homosexuality in its ranks? Isn't the anti-establishment petulance of the most vocal members of the gay community out of place in the one organization that cannot and must not tolerate disruption? Marc Wolf's great accomplishment in *Another American* is that he takes what seems merely a silly political compromise, fleshes out a complicated and legitimately contentious debate, and returns the audience to a state resembling mental clarity. J. Harris, an effeminate Army private in Vietnam ("I never really had no full masculine walk"), tells Wolf how he became the company mascot, Mary Alice, strutting around camp in jungle boots and shorts cut so high his butt cheeks were hanging out. "I picked the morale right up, as Mary Alice," he laughs.

>There were eleven of us, and .....
>>oh wait a second [*Chokes up*.]
>
>Eleven guys were in my bunker? ...
>and they all pulled through,
>>all eleven.
>
>And I – I just said
>>I just think it was me that pulled 'em all through.
>I really do yeah,
>>I kept 'em all laughing –
>>>and we cried together too
>>>>and that's OK.

[2003]

Light Hitters

In A.R. Gurney's autobiographical play *Labor Day*, the author's alter ego is described by his son as "not fundamentally a heavy hitter." The character writes moderately successful comedies and witty dramas that never clear the fence – i.e., never earn a full home run's worth of adulation or remuneration. "He hits singles or doubles primarily," the son laments.

Of course, a batter who routinely smacks base hits is a valuable asset to a team. But that fact can be overlooked in a culture cowed by publicity, self-importance, and statistical greatness – all of which obscure theater's cathartic purpose. Throughout a prolific writing career spanning forty years, Gurney has stuck to his primary task: entertaining the audience. He may not lead the league in home runs, but his finest plays – *The Dining Room*, *The Cocktail Hour* – reside in the Valhalla of works which may one day re-emerge as widely admired "classics" but, if not, still exist as perfect human creations delighting anyone who chances upon them.

Gurney's most recent play, *Ancestral Voices* (Broadway Play Publishing, 2000), mines familiar territory – the Cheeveresque world of East Coast WASPs – for an emotionally involving narrative and nuggets of polished wit. According to the introduction to the published text, this work overcame a number of obstacles on its way to the stage; most significantly, it survived its initial failure as a novel (rejected by the major New York publishing houses). "I finally arrived at the hybrid form we have here," the author reports, "part play and part narrative, designed to be read aloud by five actors." Gurney's most popular work, *Love Letters*, lent itself to stunt casting; the text was recited straight off the page by actors of whom no memorization was demanded. *Ancestral Voices* would seem to allow for the same parachuting in of stars who read their scripts off music stands. "The actors could memorize their lines," Gurney concedes, "but that would seem slightly silly within the minimalist form we arrived at."

The play tells the story of a wealthy family from Buffalo, NY, who endure the fallout of divorce, just as the country heads into World War II. The clan's elderly matriarch abruptly dumps her husband so she can marry his former best friend. An explicit comparison is drawn between the divorcée and young Catherine Earnshaw from *Wuthering Heights*. "She'd married the wrong man," the grandmother explains. "So her spirit withered away." Determined not to suffer the same fate any longer, Gram abandons the "perfectly nice man" she wed in her twenties and takes up with her own Heathcliff: a surly, arrogant fellow who treats her more carelessly than did her first husband.

The play's narrator, the adolescent grandson Eddie, hopes his grandparents will reconcile, but he is told by William McKaye, the loyal Scotsman long in the family's employ, that "once they've flown the coop you can catch them and put them back on the perch, but they never set easy again." Gram never does return to Gramp, who self-pityingly compares himself to their rust-belt metropolis, which is losing its usefulness and slipping in the rankings from the sixth to thirteenth and, finally, fifty-second largest city in the nation. Eddie's father, Harvey, believes his father-in-law's problem may be an overabundance of inherited wealth. He suggests to his wife, Jane, that the reason her father has no bounce left, no resilience to withstand such an abandonment, is he's always had it too easy in life. "You inherited money," Jane counters. "Just enough to make me want more," Harvey replies.

The breakup alarms Jane most of all. She sees the family, if not disintegrating, then stagnating. "We're becoming like – Europeans!" she shouts in a panic. Still, the reconfigured family continues to meet for a meal every weekend, minus Gramp.

> JANE: (*To Harvey*) Here goes another Sunday.
> HARVEY: Make the most of it, sweetie.
> JANE: Anna Karenina at least had the good sense to get out of town.
> EDDIE: Who's Anna Karenina?
> HARVEY: I thought you were playing croquet.
> EDDIE: Gram asked me to wait here. Who's Anna Karenina?
> HARVEY: You'll read about her when we send you away to school.

In A.R. Gurney's world, children are treated with firmness and reprimanded in a nearly adult manner for interrupting, smarting off, or – in Eddie's case – eavesdropping. The author frequently has characters of various generations perform an amusing balancing act of coldness and affection. Yet the family takes ultimate precedence, no matter how dispersed or oddly formulated, or with what stiffness siblings and spouses treat each other. Ancestors are compared to spawning salmon who reappear at their original breeding grounds, in time for death and the inevitable return to the soil if nothing else. "Family comes first," Jane scolds an adult Eddie in a brief coda to the play. "You might remind your children of that." Darwinian instincts, then, triumph in the end over competing assertions – "queer," Brontëesque, whatever – meant to redefine or disassemble the beleaguered family and its ties of blood.

Or so the characters assert. I'm not sure I believe it, or that even the playwright, haunted though he is by "ancestral voices," fully believes it. But what matters here is less the destination of the play, if we can determine that, than the ride. Once again Gurney has given us a pleasurable experience that few other playwrights can match. The tartness of the dialogue, the skillful recreation of place and time, and, most important, the affection the audience develops for the characters strike the ball out of the infield, if not the park. I said few playwrights can match Gurney's accomplishments, yet when reading or attending his plays I do not mentally rank him against his most exalted contemporaries – I merely enjoy. Or, as Pauline Kael once put it, I "bliss out."

The day I read *Proof* (Faber and Faber, 2001), David Auburn's Pulitzer Prize- and Tony Award-winning drama, *The New York Times* reported that Susannah McCorkle, the esteemed cabaret singer, jumped out the window of her 16th-floor Manhattan apartment, leaving a suicide note. Six years previous, her father – similarly afflicted with bipolar depression – suffocated himself with a plastic bag.

It was a bit spooky in this context to approach Auburn's play about a father and daughter who seem to share a tendency toward mental instability (as well as rare intellectual gifts). "Just because I went bughouse doesn't mean you will," Robert assures his daughter, Catherine, on her twenty-fifth birthday. But Robert is dead. This is a mere apparition berating his daughter for her lethargy, imploring her to use her singular talents, but also handing her a very solid bottle of champagne with which to toast her birthday. The implications are clear: Catherine may be destined to follow in his footsteps to intellectual greatness, or insanity. Or both.

Years earlier, Robert was a brilliant mathematician at the University of Chicago, famous at a young age for his contributions to game theory, algebraic geometry, and nonlinear operator theory. Unlike the characters in Michael Frayn's *Copenhagen*, Robert is an entirely fictional creation; special pleading is therefore required to establish his greatness. "He revolutionized the field twice before he was twenty-two," we are told.

Catherine spent her young adulthood caring for her widowed father, to save him from institutionalization, while her older sister Claire pursued a lucrative career in New York and paid the bills. Now Claire wants to sell the house out from under Catherine and move her back East where she can monitor her sister's mental state and, in necessary, find her psychiatric care.

Auburn could easily have made Claire an ogre – that is, even more of a bourgeois shrew – and championed Catherine, the unstable genius, at Claire's expense. And, indeed, there are some amusing exchanges of dialogue where our sympathies are directed toward the younger sister, as when she sarcastically acquiesces to Claire's plans.

> CATHERINE: I'm going to sit quietly on the plane to New York. And live quietly in a cute apartment. And answer Dr. Von Heimlich's questions very politely.
> CLAIRE: You can see any doctor you like, or you can see no doctor.
> CATHERINE: I would like to see a doctor called Dr. Von Heimlich: please find one. And I would like him to wear a monocle. And I'd like him to have a very soft, very well-upholstered couch, so that I'll be perfectly comfortable while I'm blaming everything on you.

But Claire is in a difficult, adult position: she has responsibilities for her sister's well-being that justify a bit of coercion. Catherine's mental state is uncertain. The same holds for Robert in two flashback scenes, during a brief period of recovery. This has important implications for the plot because, separate from the cache of notebooks filled with copious jottings that Robert left behind (Catherine: "It's gibberish."), there is one containing a lucid mathematical theorem that Catherine claims as her own. The ambiguity surrounding her sanity, and her father's insanity, taints her claim to authorship.

Auburn makes one sound decision after another here. I especially liked that the play is not ultimately about the fraudulent nature of truth. That is, the author doesn't abscond with ideas from science – uncertainty, relativity – and misapply them to this episode in Catherine's professional life. There is an absolute truth here. Catherine either did or did not write the theorem.

It is also a welcome development that mental illness is never romanticized. Its onset does not unlock brilliant ideas from the minds of the afflicted; rather, it destroys Robert's career, makes nonsense of his life, and hijacks the life of his younger daughter. Only in the humanities, where the greatness of a foolish idea can be asserted through a diligent PR campaign, does insanity retain its chic appeal. In the sciences, madness turns the mind to mush.

Finally, Auburn resists the temptation to allow one of the characters to burn the only extant copy of the impossible-to-memorize proof. That shows admirable restraint. It is also somewhat daring to allude to Sophie Germain, the nineteenth century Frenchwoman who, denied access to formal university training because of her sex, became a formidable mathematical theoretician all the same. The implications about Catherine's life are actually the reverse: her brilliant work – for indeed it is hers – was facilitated, not slowed, by a withdrawal from university necessitated by her father's relapse. Burdened with no social or professional life, and with plenty of time on her hands, Catherine got to work.

The author develops a mood of pervasive sadness, not merely at the implosion of at least one productive mind, but at the recurrent phenomenon of talented persons peaking early in life. (Both Robert and Catherine seem doomed to do their best work in their early 20s.) And I found touching the modesty of the play's fourth character, Hal, a former student of Robert's, and Catherine's love interest. A self-proclaimed mathematical mediocrity, he gives the play, with all its talk of brilliance and genius, some welcome grounding. Mercifully, Catherine finds this nonprodigy – her intellectual inferior – "not boring."

The important awards Auburn received for this play elicited predictable sniping from critics claiming that industry accolades are inevitably bestowed on safe, harmless products (not the work of heavy hitters). In fact, awards seem to function most often as gratuitous confirmation of the self-important, politically preordained "home runs" that dominate media coverage of the arts. (In the wake of *The Vagina Monologues*, Eve Ensler was awarded a Guggenheim Fellowship.) *Proof* is the sort of well-constructed, intelligent entertainment that, were it the rule rather than the exception in theater, would contribute to a growing pool of fine dramatic works from which emerges a culture's true greatness.

I should have warmed to David Lindsay-Abaire's *Fuddy Meers* (Overlook, 2001) if only because it ridicules my bête noire: the absurd Christian notion of instant forgiveness and redemption – a system of moral amnesia that permits one to duck responsibility for sins and cruelties through sincere repentance. "Of course, you can't really ever escape who you are and what you've done," the author, risking blasphemy, tells Celia Wren in an interview from 2000. "Aren't we all destined to re-create our lives every day, relive our mistakes?"

Lindsay-Abaire set out to write a play about persons trying to forget dubious pasts "plus one person who needed to remember." That one person is Claire, a trusting wife and mother with a sunny disposition who suffers from a neurological disorder, a clinical amnesia by which she awakens each morning with no memory of what went before. This affliction permits less principled characters – a husband and ex-husband – to exploit Claire's vulnerability by denying histories of violence.

"I did something very bad," confesses Claire's current spouse, Richard, out of earshot of Claire, "and I've never paid for it." All he can do now is remake himself in the Norman Rockwell image of a devoted family man who instructs his clueless wife on what style of clothing she likes, what beverage she prefers. "This is very unsettling," Claire decides for what must be the several hundredth time she's risen from bed to find this cheerful enforcer of consumer false consciousness leading her by the nose.

But today is different: no sooner does Richard step out to shower than a manacled man in a ski mask, who both limps and lisps, crawls out from under the bed and implores Claire to run away with him. "That man in the shower ith going to kill you, Claire," he insists. "He'th a very dangeroth perthon." Faced with death, or at best the soullessness of middle-class conventionality, Claire acquiesces. The Limping Man then drives her, for no logical reason, to her mother's house, where they meet up with accomplices. Claire's teenage son Kenny and Richard are also in hot pursuit. Mayhem ensues.

Lindsay-Abaire admits to tinkering with the script like a Rube Goldberg contraption. "*Fuddy Meers* is a ride," he explains in the introduction to the trade paperback. The title itself – one character's mispronunciation of "funny mirrors" – is a reference to the disorienting sensations of a traveling carnival, with its exhilarating roller coasters and tilt-a-whirls manned by frightening ex-cons. There is a cartoon element to the play that is quite explicit: one of the Limping Man's accomplices speaks through a hand puppet, which is straight out of *South Park*; other characters are assigned distinctive "comic" speech impediments, just like the Warner Bros. animal menagerie (Porky Pig, Tweetie Bird, Sylvester). The script can be read as an inversion of the film *Groundhog Day*, or yet another text influenced by Quentin Tarantino, whose films, when not obsessed with movie violence, explore the intricacies of narrative structure.

But, clearly, the author's greatest influence is playwright Christopher Durang, with whom Lindsay-Abaire studied at Juilliard. "I don't think there's been a piece written about me that hasn't mentioned the fact that he and I live in the same world," Lindsay-Abaire states defensively to Celia Wren. But with their shared fondness for manic characters, illogically comic dialogue, and eruptions of violence, the comparison is unavoidable, particularly since Lindsay-Abaire filled a previous play, *A Devil Inside*, with allusions to the same Russian novels Durang referenced in *The Idiots Karamazov*. To me, comparisons between playwrights are useful, not dismissive. But I seem to be the rare author who does not fear the term *derivative* as the most loathsome pejorative. A number of fiction writers whom I quite enjoy – Peter Cameron, Ann Beattie – owe a great deal to J.D. Salinger, whose work echoes Saroyan, who updated the ingratiating vernacular of *Huck Finn*. The "originals" in literature – Beckett, I suppose, or William S. Burroughs – seem often to be huffing and puffing a bit too hard, to the reader's detriment.

My hesitation to embrace *Fuddy Meers*, then, does not spring from a dismissal of the work as being too much like *Baby with the Bathwater* or *The Vietnamization of New Jersey*. (Would it even be possible to write a script that is not, in some fundamental way, original to the author?) My reservations stem from the mixed purposes of the piece. "I'm trying to write outrageous farce with an underlying sadness," Lindsay-Abaire explains to Wren. In the play's introduction, the author gratefully acknowledges collaborators at the Manhattan Theatre Club who "understood that the play could be whimsical and silly, and still be very real and painful at its center." My objection is this: if you decide to build a thrill ride, you should try to build a perfect thrill ride, not a thrill ride that elicits deep feeling. A Rube Goldberg contraption with a melancholy soul is not a pretty piece of work.

Lindsay-Abaire makes things hard enough for himself by placing his writing in an unsavory, ersatz genre: male heterosexual camp. He compounds that problem by attempting tonal shifts which are nearly impossible to pull off. Even Durang rarely succeeds at that.

Playwrights would be well advised to perfect the silliness of a silly narrative, à la Joe Orton, Jennifer Saunders in her *Absolutely Fabulous* television scripts, and Oscar Wilde with *The Importance of Being Earnest*. As it turns out, sadness and pain are unavoidable in any dramatic work because theater is a collaborative undertaking among mere mortals: every performer and audience member will one day suffer and die, or just die. One can write with that thought foremost, using either a somber or comedic tone, or one can construct a diversion – a thrill ride – that bravely and irresponsibly disregards our ultimate fate. But mixing the two approaches is rarely a good idea.

In the play's final scene, Kenny and Richard try in vain to stop Claire from napping so as not to lose the familiarity and affection that's been building since dawn. But sentimentality does not belong here. Ironically, there is no payoff to *Fuddy Meers* because the author tries too hard to make it resonate.

Like A.R. Gurney's dramatic oeuvre, Lanford Wilson's work spans nearly four decades and boasts no home runs. The difference is Wilson's plays have been less consistently successful on their own aesthetic terms. *The Hot L Baltimore*, *Fifth of July*, and *Talley's Folly* have had their impact but, to extend the baseball metaphor, Wilson's batting average is, I would say, a full hundred points below Gurney's.

The Broadway-hostile cast of twelve in Wilson's latest work, *Book of Days* (Grove, 2000), implies the author accepts his place in regional, university, and Off-Broadway theater. Set "on the cusp of a new millennium" in Dublin, Missouri – a prosperous berg with fewer than 5,000 inhabitants – the play spirals around in time to relate the moralistic tale of the town's Casanova (a budding politician) who gets away with double murder despite the hysterical accusations of a Joan of Arc wannabe.

Ruth Hoch, bookkeeper at the local cheese plant, is about to take on the title role of Shaw's *Saint Joan* and, a bit belatedly, assume Joan's anti-clerical stance, though she is clearly "all wrong" for the part, just as tiny Dublin, MO, is all wrong for the setting of this play, which features a theater company whose productions of classical drama – helmed by "a big-time Broadway director" – enjoy five-week runs.

Wilson employs cast members as a chorus to move the action along. The language used is pretty stale at times. For example, we are told of an athletic hero who, "cool as a cucumber" and with "ice water in his veins," found "nothing but nylon" scoring a winning basket some years ago. The countryside surrounding Dublin is described mostly in sentence fragments:

> EARL: The Ozark Mountains.
> SHARON: Lakes and rivers
> SHERIFF ATKINS: Great fishing
> WALT: The whole countryside so beautiful in the spring it could break your heart
> LOUANN: Dogwood trees
> GINGER: Redbud
> EARL: Dairy farms
> BOYD: The grass so green it hurts your eyes

I've lived in and around the lush countrysides of rural Wisconsin, Stockholm's archipelago, the Shenandoah Valley, and the Finger Lakes region of upstate New York, and never has the intense green coloring hurt my eyes. Why does Wilson write like that? And what possesses a playwright to include among his characters one free-spirited woman who conceived her first child, stoned, at Woodstock? Has he no inkling we've heard it all before?

At other times, the dialogue in *Book of Days* is rather sharp.

> REVEREND GROVES: Miss Reed, I believe that's the shortest skirt that ever walked into this church.
> GINGER: It shrunk in the wash.

And there is one brilliant passage where the first murder victim's wife refuses to perform her grieving-widow scene; a fellow cast member is forced to act as understudy and play her breakdown for her. I also appreciated the implications of a subplot, integral to the play's main action, in which the cheese plant manager convinces the wealthy owner to withhold a fraction of his output from their main client, a dairy conglomerate that produces the rubberized goods we see on supermarket shelves. Len, the manager, promises his boss a more savory cheese a few years down the road, as well as the possibility of greater profits. It's worth the risk, he assures him, and besides, "you got all the money you're ever gonna need." In other countries, Wilson implies, people are poor enough to eat delicious meals, whereas Americans must first pass through a zone of comfortable wealth and arrive at absolutely appalling riches before we begin to consider the merits of pleasurable eating.

In other words, *Book of Days* is not entirely bereft of interesting ideas, effective scenes, or amusing dialogue. But neither does it consistently deliver them. This play is like a sacrifice fly that performs the necessary work of moving the team into scoring position, for next time. Most bothersome for me is the local

Joan of Arc character, Ruth, particularly during a phony fit of paranoid hysteria in which her identify merges with Joan's and she remains involuntarily in character. (I realize this is the sort of shtick actors love, but it embarrasses the rest of us.) "Something's not right," Ruth announces early on, when an accidental shooting triggers suspicions of foul play. She sets out on a sleuthing mission worthy of Angela Lansbury or Dick Van Dyke, made possible only by the implausible bumbling of local authorities. By the time she arrives at her climactic anti-clerical scene ("your counsel is of the devil"), I had lost all sympathy for her. Though a member of the Episcopal church in a neighboring city, Ruth challenges church authority at a fundamentalist congregation in Dublin. Thus, she is nothing like Joan of Arc, who was martyred and later canonized by the same officious hierarchy to which she owed allegiance. Rather, Ruth is an Anglican snob looking down her nose at the local yokels, whose house of worship she invades and desecrates. In short, I found her sanctimonious behavior offensive, which is a deadly development. An unsympathetic Joan is no Joan at all.

[2002]

Scary Balding White Men in Suits: Anna Deavere Smith Talks to Us

"Acting is the farthest thing from lying that I have encountered," asserts actress and playwright Anna Deavere Smith in her new memoir. "It is the most unfake thing there is."

But the opposite paradox is equally telling: we are most untruthful when posing as ourselves. This accounts for the difficulties Smith faced developing her most recent play, *House Arrest* – a "work in progress" that became a group discussion and, numerous drafts later, took final form as a three-hundred-page book, *Talk to Me: Listening Between the Lines* (Random House, 2000). Through its several configurations, *House Arrest* never came together as a satisfying scripted work for the theater. Smith's previous two plays – *Fires in the Mirror* and *Twilight: Los Angeles, 1992* – captured cities in the grip of racial unrest so effectively that the playwright's success corrupted the research process for subsequent works. Smith now faces interview subjects who know the fate of their predecessors and perform accordingly, or refuse to speak at all.

Compounding that problem was the choice of subject matter. In fall 1993, while performing *Fires in the Mirror* at Arena Stage in Washington, D.C., Smith was approached about writing a new play. "How about if I do something on the president?" Smith asked Arena's artistic director. "He has to be in the press so much. I wonder how he has time to do his work."

That childlike observation somehow passed muster. So, rather then pursue more promising topics outside Washington – the plight of incarcerated women, a rash of church burnings in the South – Smith accepted Arena Stage's commission and launched the "Press and Presidency Project," ensuring that her potential interview subjects (members of the press, and government employees who had at least a passing familiarity with the author and her politically charged plays) refused to cooperate or, if they did consent to an interview, generated some of the least genuine language imaginable – as befits their training.

This was a lamentable slip in judgment by Smith, who has spent nearly two decades shaping plays and giving performances based on actual events in a series titled *On the Road: A Search for American Character*. This larger project and Smith's method of fashioning dramatic works entirely from interview transcripts had their genesis in 1981. "I wanted to hear – well – authentic speech," Smith writes of her original epiphany, "speech that you could dance to, speech that had the possibility of breaking through the walls of the listener, speech that could get to your heart, and beyond that to someplace else in your consciousness." Accumulating a library of tapes, Smith listened with great care to her subjects' language as well as to their pauses and breaths – verbal tics she likened to the embellishments of a jazz musician. "I think it's about finding that moment when syntax changes," she concluded of her methodology, "when grammar breaks down." It was those moments she felt she had to study to know who a person really was.

Grammatical and syntactical shifts can prove revealing in the emotionally naked voice of a stabbing victim's grieving brother. But members of the Eastern media elite and their political subjects use guarded language from which Smith failed to elicit compelling revelations or jazz-like riffs, if the surviving interviews in *Talk to Me* are a reliable indication.

For example: apropos of an earlier president abused by the press, slaveholder Thomas Jefferson, documentarian Ken Burns insists – plausibly – that chattel slavery was a dehumanizing institution. "Now tell me how long you would like to live under this [system]?" he asks rhetorically, working himself into a less-than-spontaneous frenzy.

> I would say a generation's too long
> a decade's too long, a year is too long,
> a month is too long, a week's too long.
> I submit if you were asked to do that
> you might try it on for twenty minutes.

Prepared speech passed off as impromptu dialogue reveals something about the speaker. But Burns' egregiously stagy oration, on a point no one contests, is self-congratulatory and deadening. "We gave up, finally, on the idea of a traditional play," Smith writes in a section of her memoir dated Spring 1999. Had the impeachment process not already pushed the Clinton presidency into utter banality, Smith's theater piece most likely would have failed just the same. The author seems to have stepped into the "Press and Presidency Project" burdened with an impulsive, starry-eyed naïveté; she never gains a clear view of the man who held our highest office. Smith concludes her analysis: "Perhaps Clinton's downfall was that he was too expressive in a time when studied nonchalance is the status quo." Clinton's troubles, in fact, were a great deal more complicated than that, and Smith's bloated project – with its three-room staffed command center, its hefty expense account, and its consulting firm – never made much progress toward unearthing the layers of truth.

"Washington once sat on a swamp," Smith notes, repeating the most trite observation an outsider can make about the city. "Now it sits, I think, upon the patriarchy. It is the grandest of patriarchal structures."

Grander than the Vatican? Smith misses entirely the irony of Bill Clinton's saga. It was his own political party and his avid feminist supporters – not the "scary balding white men in suits" Smith sees lurking behind every door – who succeeded in moving sex into the public sphere. (The personal is now political.) More perplexing still is Smith's silence on the fundamental disconnect between a stage technique that stalls in the absence of honest language and a subject who based his defense on a legalistic ruse. Among the hundreds of persons Smith interviewed, someone must have pointed this out to her. But the author of *Talk to Me* is not the same Anna Deavere Smith who enjoyed success with *Fires in the*

Mirror and *Twilight* by taking a broad view of events, inhabiting her subjects on stage, unreservedly loving every character, and allowing each his or her say. Here, the author is a single voice prone to pronouncements, as when she attributes racist motives to Maureen Dowd of *The New York Times* when the columnist acts juvenile and petty.

For that reason, I would rather have available a published script of *House Arrest*, in any of its staged versions, than this memoir. Among the interview excerpts included here is a vivid two-page narrative by Penny Kiser, a tour guide at Monticello whose work places her outside the hermetic echo of the East Coast media corridor. And Secretary of Labor Alexis Herman recounts a childhood ambush by the Ku Klux Klan on a Southern back road, when her father handed her a loaded gun. ("Oh yeah. I was tiny.") But compelling revelations about the project's designated subject – the press and the presidency – are extremely rare. Newspaper columnist Walter Shapiro does offer a useful explanation of how the media honeymoon for President-elect Clinton was aborted in November 1992 when reporters who had covered the unsuccessful Bush campaign, newly reassigned, descended on Little Rock "loaded for bear." And numerous observers lament a journalistic climate that keeps the attention of media personnel focused on scandals, gaffs, and humiliations or, most exciting of all, a possible assassination attempt that could ignite a reporter's career. Everybody, in other words, is on "the deathwatch" and hoping for the worst.

[2002]

Where Arthur Miller Stands

Arthur Miller's reputation for fierce independence and keen virtue would seem beyond question. He has been admired for opposing early on America's disastrous military campaign in Indochina. As president of International PEN, he rebuked the head of the Soviet Writers Union, Alexei Surkov, when the Russian suggested that the world organization gut its censorship statutes. And though Miller's own government deemed renewal of his passport not to be in the country's best interests in 1953, he has never seemed to waver in his admiration for the U.S. Constitution and what he calls the "miraculous rationalism of the American Bill of Rights." Most famously, perhaps, Miller refused to cooperate with the House Un-American Activities Committee, which found him in contempt. By resisting the demands of this group of legislators, Miller became a hero. The episode stands as a defining indication of his public character, most notably among those inclined to accept as simple fact Hollywood's subsequent routine representation of the period as utterly unambiguous in moral terms.

But there is an unwelcome cloud darkening any assessment of Miller's intellectual career, a nagging cough that distracts attention from the chorus of praise Miller enjoys regarding his "majestic stature," to quote the late novelist Joseph Heller, and his "habitual dedication to justice, mercy, dignity, and truth." It's a familiar story: Miller was snookered by socialist utopianism prior to the 1950s, when forced starvation and other forms of mass murder were intruding on the Soviet workers' paradise, and reports of show trials, implausible confessions, and absurd conspiracy theories were emanating from Moscow. This does not set Miller apart from any number of gullible intellectuals and artists of the period, but that's the point: regarding the most significant ideological sham of the century, Miller was no more clear-sighted, no less self-deluded than the majority.

It is instructive that British socialist George Orwell – a writer immune to what C.M. Woodhouse calls "the demagogues' claptrap about equality" – achieved fame with an anti-Soviet fable. Orwell set out on the arduous task of finding a publisher for *Animal Farm* in 1943, when military pragmatism dictated the accordance of American and British forces with the Stalinist regime, and Orwell's message, therefore, was least welcome. In direct contrast, Miller was puzzled and appalled by the sudden turn in public opinion against our former ally, the Red Army, following the end of the war. As late as 1949, at the Cultural and Scientific Conference for World Peace in New York, Miller heard automaton Dmitri Shostakovich recite an affirmation of the peaceful intentions of his persecutors among the Soviet leadership, after which the playwright ironically renewed his commitment to "resisting the burgeoning new anti-Soviet crusade."

Hindsight, as we know, is 20/20, and I am aware that I would be well-advised to keep in mind the economic uncertainty under which Miller and his generation were living when they arrived at their Communist sympathies, and the gratitude Americans – particularly Jewish Americans – felt immediately after the war toward the Soviets for repelling the Nazi onslaught on the Eastern front. But in his 1999 lecture *"The Crucible* in History," Miller persists in expressing dismay at the rapidity with which the Soviet Union shifted from ally to enemy, suggesting that a clear understanding of the period and its political dynamic eludes the author to this day.

Miller took numerous missteps during a confusing period — so have we all — but he compounds those errors by sounding defensive about his poor judgment, remaining officially unrepentant, and in some ways clinging to an unenlightened position. "[H]aving once been pro-Soviet," Miller complains about having to defend his record, "I had failed later on to make the right exculpatory noises, the passionate anti-Soviet protestations." In the 1995 introduction to a reissued edition of *Timebends*, he concludes that his autobiography — so highly regarded in Europe and Latin America — was passed over or attacked in the United States due to "a protracted animus in some American commentators for anyone who was attracted by Marxism and what once seemed the promise of a more benign Russian socialist civilization."

I understand why the author would be miffed by the muted reception to *Timebends*, which is an impressive literary achievement. But Miller's obstinacy is unseemly: he ignored all warning signs and backed the wrong horse, full stop. No one likes to face up to mistakes made in good faith, but with his defensive posturing Miller risks belittling crimes committed on a monumental scale. "I can't think of how to apologize," he insists.

And yet, Miller makes what sound very much like soothing exculpatory noises throughout *Timebends* and other works of nonfiction. "If the one-party Soviet system seemed doubtfully democratic," he writes of his early enthusiasm for Stalinism, "there was plenty of denial available to turn the gaze away." Fascism and Nazism, he allows, were imitations of Soviet forms. In "Miracles," from 1973, he observes, "How often have I heard survivors of the Thirties astonished that they could have said the things they said, believed what they believed." And he condemns his generation's hope of finding a higher ethic in the Soviet Union as "a worldwide irony of catastrophic moral proportions."

Most significantly, Miller suggests that by supporting "a paranoid and murderous Stalinist regime," Western intellectuals were abetting its crimes. An important distinction must be drawn, then: Miller *has* apologized, his protestations notwithstanding; but he is unwilling to admit having done so, because that would resemble too closely the act of public capitulation he resisted during the McCarthy Era — a phenomenon he dismisses as "the spectacle of the born-again anti-Soviet ex-radical" who lies on his back "wailing his guilty remorse for his errors." Over time, Miller changed his beliefs and shifted his allegiances, but he remains hesitant to acknowledge the extent of that change and its implications, or willing to do so *only on his own terms*, which is precisely what serves to elicit deep admiration for the man.

But it also introduces ambiguities in his relationship to "justice, mercy, dignity, and truth" — ambiguities that are not clarified by the pieces collected in *Echoes Down the Corridor* (Viking, 2000), which comprises thirty-eight essays published by

Miller since 1944 (but not included in the expanded 1996 edition of his *Theater Essays*), plus five excerpts from previously published books of reportage. Two essays from the mid-60s – "The Nazi Trials and the German Heart" and "Guilt and *Incident in Vichy*" – examine the aftermath of Nazism in Germany and consider the lingering ties between the Nazi regime and the German people. Miller grows justifiably incensed at the suggestion that his journalistic work on the war-crimes trials is unfair to the post-war Germans, or that he is giving Germany a "bad name." He responds: "Surely, if the German police had picked up a twenty-two-man gang that had tortured and killed merely for money, or even for kicks, an outcry would go up from the Germans, a demand that justice be done. Why is there this uneasy silence at best, and this resentment at worst, excepting that in the Frankfurt cases these accused worked for a state under its orders?"

Replace "German" with "Russian," and you get a good idea of what is missing from this collection: a consideration of the lingering ties between the Russian people and the Stalinist regime they and the American intelligentsia embraced. "Perhaps the deepest respect we can pay the millions of innocent dead," Miller concludes about the Nazi atrocities, "is to examine what we believe about murder, and our responsibility as survivors for the future." It seems to me Miller's greatest responsibility is to those victims whose murders he admits to effectively abetting. He is able to report from a courtroom in Frankfurt during a trial of twenty-two Hitler SS men because Germany circa 1964 was an open society taking steps toward self-examination. He cannot report from a courtroom in Perm or Sverdlovsk because, after Khrushchëv denounced the excesses of his predecessor, the petty masters of Stalin's barbed-wire world were never put on trial. That is a significant nondevelopment worthy of Miller's deepest concern and condemnation.

"Nothing escapes Miller's piercing scrutiny," promises editor Steven R. Centola in the collection's prefatory note, "as he discusses such subjects as the Holocaust, the Nazi War Crimes Trials, the Great Depression, the Cold War, McCarthyism, the Vietnam War, anti-Semitism, censorship, juvenile delinquency, the Watergate scandal, capital punishment, and the oppression of dissident writers in foreign countries." But one significant development does escape Miller's piercing scrutiny in his role as "chronicler of the historical procession of the twentieth century": the mass terror induced by a government he was enamored of.

Let me make clear: I take issue with Miller to protect the historical record – which has gained stark confirmation from the newly opened Soviet archives – but I also question the adoration in which admirers shroud one of our most successful playwrights. Because he defied Congressional interrogators and challenged their footmen in the field, Miller is widely viewed as the conscience of the writing community – the one righteous man in Sodom. But supporters, once they are wedded to this husbandly writer, project onto him the false image of a perfect moral barometer. That is wrong, and that is dangerous – for Miller – because when mere mortals are worshiped as gods they have no reason to hold themselves to high standards anymore. And *Echoes Down the Corridor* shows us an essayist suffering from low standards.

Leaving aside failed satirical pieces like "Let's Privatize Congress" and "A Modest Proposal for the Pacification of the Public Temper," which are nearly impossible to pull off, a significant number of the essays assembled here are poorly argued in simple rhetorical terms. "The Good Old American Apple Pie," for example, announces in 1993 that a new wave of censorship is threatening American artists and writers. But the author cites only one specific case of contemporary censorship: "right now," he claims, "some three hundred and fifty lines of *Romeo and Juliet* are customarily removed from American school textbooks because they are about sex." Miller fails to establish if even this single example – of a writer whose unexpurgated works are available in every public library – is a new development or a longstanding editorial policy that suggests nothing at all about the political climate of 1993.

In "On True Identity" from 1975, Miller takes issue with Frances Knight, a U.S. government official, for her proposal that every American carry an identity card, which Miller compares to the internal passports required "under the czars," "under the Soviets now," "in South Africa," and "in Nazi Germany." What he neglects to acknowledge is that numerous social democracies employ a secure I.D. system of a nature similar to what Ms. Knight proposes to combat crime and protect generous entitlement programs against double dipping and other corruption – with a minimum of fascist oppression. Such lapses in argumentation, obvious to the reader but passed over by the author, make this and a number of other essays ineffectual as serious, persuasive documents.

Least persuasive is "Dinner with the Ambassador," which recounts a trip Miller made to Turkey with Harold Pinter on behalf of the International PEN organization in 1985. (It was official U.S. policy at the time to support the Turkish regime, a military ally, while enticing its leaders with carrots in hopes of easing the government's crackdown on dissidents. Miller and Pinter favored the use of sticks.)

Miller gives a detailed account of the U.S. Embassy dinner held on the occasion of his visit and attended by Turkish journalists and political figures outside the government. After Ambassador Robert Strausz-Hupe toasts the guest of honor, Miller responds with an impolitic speech attacking the dismal human rights situation in the host country: the military government may be taking steps toward democratization, but it is still a violent dictatorship, and so on. "As I continued," Miller narrates with less than complete reliability, "I thought I saw the eyes of the ambassador glaze with astonishment and horror." Afterwards, Strausz-Hupe thanks Miller for a fascinating evening. "This is one you won't forget soon," Miller assures him. Finally as the guests are collecting to leave, Harold Pinter deliberately insults the host, who chides him for his vulgar language. Pinter is elated by the rebuke, which he immediately relates to his friend. "We decided we ought to form a team that would visit American embassies around the world," Miller reports.

I recognize this sort of behavior from my high school days, when classmates trying to impress the rebellious crowd would taunt the principal until he lost his cool. But it is beneath the dignity of major literary figures to carry on this way. And I believe they wouldn't dare to if only their colleagues, academics, and members of the media held them to basic standards of adult behavior, rather than showering them with unearned hosannas for their "courage."

Significantly, Miller maintains a stronger relationship to sustained moral questioning and intellectual rigor in his stage work – *The Crucible* and *Incident at Vichy* retain their white-hot intensity and power nearly a half century on – and it is on stage that the author has conducted his most honest self-examination. I refer specifically to the 1986 one-act collection titled, appropriately, *Danger: Memory!*

Comprising "I Can't Remember Anything" and "Clara," *Danger: Memory!* resonates with Miller's own life and the experiences of his entire generation of intellectuals. The male lead in "I Can't Remember Anything," an elderly man named Leo, is a lifelong Communist who must ignore or forget everything he has witnessed over the years in order to retain his political faith. The pervading mood is defeatist – greed, vile habits, and Richard Nixon are understood to have conquered the nation. Left unsaid is the fact that Communism proved inherently bankrupt and in its service idealism was the worst betrayer of all. "[W]hy can't you just admit that it's all nothing?" Leo is asked by Leonora, a widowed friend whose history, like her name, parallels his own. "You *know* it's nothing, Leo."

> LEO: (*stalling*) What's nothing?
> LEONORA: Why, our lives, the whole damned thing.

In "Clara," an idealistic young social worker is found murdered. Willful denial cost Clara Kroll her life: she became romantically involved with a prisoner client who had killed a previous girlfriend. Albert Kroll blames himself for his daughter's fatal career choice and her trusting nature. After discovering the bloody corpse, he is unable to cooperate with the police investigator, Lieutenant Fine.

> FINE: Generally – you probably know – we block things we're ashamed to remember.
> KROLL: I know.
> FINE: Things that make us feel guilty, you know what I mean?

The detective later explodes with impatience.

> FINE: [I]t's your lies you can't let go of. It's ten, twenty, thirty years of shit you told your daughter, to the point where she sacrificed her life, for what? – To uphold what you don't believe in yourself.

But the play ends, tellingly, with a reaffirmation of Kroll's former idealism: in Clara's catastrophe, Miller explains, Kroll "has rediscovered himself and glimpsed the tragic collapse of values that he finally cannot bring himself to renounce."

I side with Officer Fine. That is, I second his call for abandoning self-congratulatory idealism in favor of hard-nosed pragmatism, even if that means renouncing one's tragically collapsed values. (I believe this can be accomplished without flailing on one's back, or capitulating to the Joe McCarthys of the world.) More important, I suggest that we praise Miller and other literary heroes judiciously, work by work, episode by episode – for their sake as well as our own – and that we take pains to save our greatest adulation for intellectuals and artists who do not turn their gaze away in denial from brutalities that invalidate their political sympathies.

[2001]

Holding History

One could say of John Logan that he works in the Elizabethan tradition. Shakespeare and Marlowe routinely lifted dramatic plots from familiar source material – popular continental works or lurid accounts from British history. The subject of Logan's play *Never the Sinner* (Overlook, 1999) is an old tabloid chestnut and the subject of prior Hollywood treatments: the Leopold and Loeb murder trial.

Logan treats this tale of two privileged teens as a "very dark, very serpentine love story" – a love story with a corpse. Had the corpse belonged to one of the young lovers, we might feel drawn to the material for its sordid poignancy. As it is, the victim is a random bystander chosen as part of a philosophical exercise. The story's emotional appeal is thereby lost. What's left is curiosity and titillation and, I will admit, I was somewhat curious and mildly titillated.

The playwright reworked this script for fifteen years prior to the play's Off-Broadway run and publication, but he still faces basic dramaturgical problems inherent in the material. Defense attorney Clarence Darrow, fearing a death sentence for his clients from an indignant jury, counsels the accused to change their pleas to guilty, thereby placing the sentencing decision in the hands of a trial judge. Darrow then attempts to generate sympathy for his clients, who appear in court wearing expensive suits and slicked-back hair; who smirk at the dull, prodding questions of the prosecution; who misuse *whomever* while spouting Nietzsche. "It is my belief," Darrow tells the court, "that it is primary to the rendering of punishment that we understand [the murderers'] *motivations*. To do so we must begin, of course, with a complete understanding of their psychological health."

But their motivations remain perplexing, to Darrow, to their psychologists, to the court, to the playwright, and to the theater audience. Darrow explains his clients' problem thus: "somewhere ... somehow ... in the infinite processes that go into the making of a boy or a man something ... *slipped*." This is a nonexplanation. After some delay, the defense calls an expert witness who gives psychological testimony about the boys' arrested emotional development. This, too, is unilluminating.

The nagging question Logan – and Darrow – must answer, of course, is why more people with arrested emotional development don't commit murder just to prove they can. "To say that Leopold and Loeb were 'monsters' is too easy," the playwright asserts in the introduction to the published text. "To say they were 'evil' is too facile." But he continues: "They were brutal. They lacked any true moral, ethical compass. They could not find their way in our sunlit world, so they embraced the darkness." By so stating, Logan merely expounds at flowery length on the same point the rejected term *evil* would have made more succinctly.

The most intractable problem is this: Clarence Darrow engages in rhetorical gamesmanship throughout his defense. He is a gun for hire, making the argument he was paid to make, and making it well (and successfully). The playwright attributes to Darrow long, sincere pleas for compassion and understanding but neglects to examine the elements of professionalism and subterfuge weakening those pleas. As long as Logan presents Darrow's explanation as the *play's* explanation, the problem persists: we don't believe the mitigating circumstances in this sentencing hearing are exceptional any more than Darrow does. Accepting Darrow's smokescreen at face value, the playwright appears naïve. But to correct this problem, Logan would need to divert inordinate attention to a supporting character in what we are told is a love story about Leopold and Loeb.

Logan does plausibly assert that the boys committed the murder to seal an emotional bond. ("There's no going back," Leopold exclaims to his friend over the dead body. "We're together now. Forever.") He fleshes out testimony by Dr. White, a witness for the defense, with material on the pair's fantasy lives: Loeb wishes to head a criminal gang, while Leopold imagines himself the slave to a benign king. One masterminds, the other grovels; in short, each meets his own worst match. Logan shows us the fatally combustible chemistry of the pairing but, with *evil* discounted as too facile, he cannot explain the individual personalities that form this bond.

Though Leopold and Loeb were both Jewish, Logan does not include anti-Semitism in the public's hysteria during the trial. And he is sly about the sexual implications of the crime. Dr. White's testimony that Leopold, even in jail, finds Loeb's body immeasurably thrilling is crosscut with a newspaper headline: "Body of Boy Found in Swamp!" Despite Loeb's assertion that the senseless violation of societal norms is "the only thing that has a point" – as befits a Nietzschean *Übermensch* – the murderers are horrified by court discussions of their physical relationship. This is not, as some would portray it, a case of two hipsters rubbing the noses of the bourgeoisie in the dirt. Quite the opposite: Dr. White – the voice of bourgeois science and medicine – offers matter-of-fact analysis of their relationship, while the hipsters squirm.

"Does the *truth* have no value then?" Leopold sniffs when his partner suggests he assume responsibility for the blows that killed the boy. The line recalls passages from Tom Kalin's 1992 film *Swoon*, another treatment of the Leopold and Loeb case, which adopts an oddly detached view of murder until Loeb is killed by a fellow prisoner, at which point the filmmakers turn uptight and judgmental of the injustice done to one of their protagonists. Logan himself falls into no such trap of inconsistency. At worst, his appeal for balance and understanding gives rise to familiar platitudes, the most annoying of which is echoed in the title. "I can see the sin in all the world," quotes Darrow to the court some half century before evangelical Christians commenced their crusade against gay rights. "And I may well hate that sin, but never the sinner."

In contrast to Logan's meticulously factual courtroom drama, Robert O'Hara's *Insurrection: Holding History* (TCG, 1999) is a fantastic mix of inherited fable and secondhand research owing much to William Styron's *The Confessions of Nat Turner*, itself a work of imagination. Tony Kushner's influence is also asserted. We are told in the preface by the play's dramaturge, Shelby Jiggetts-Tivony, "In *Insurrection*, the gay fantasia on national themes and the colored museum of Black stereotypes collide and merge." The play's homosexual elements, however, remain entirely incidental.

The play, developed to satisfy the author's dissertation requirement at Columbia University, features a Columbia University graduate student completing his dissertation. (Not surprisingly, this is O'Hara's first play. He was twenty-six years old when it premiered at The Joseph Papp Public Theater.) Ronald Porter, visiting his family down South, learns that his surviving great-great-grandfather, the one-hundred-eighty-nine-year-old T.J., was with Nat Turner in Southampton County, Virginia, at the time of the insurrection. Ron has qualms about using the subject of slave rebellion as dissertation fodder, but the material seizes his imagination and won't let go. By virtue of time travel, T.J. is transformed into a healthy young man, and Ron becomes a prophet foretelling of Nat Turner's rebellion to the very slaves who will rebel.

O'Hara's Turner is a hatchet-wielding maniac in an agitated state of euphoria, inspired by Jesus Christ and driven by visions of the Holy Ghost. Depicting Turner's followers, O'Hara satirizes the sycophancy with which the oppressed flatter their oppressor. "WHITE MAN!" a slave named Hammet warns, interrupting the momentum of Nat Turner's call to arms. Izzie Mae, quick on her feet, begins to shout.

> IZZIE MAE: MIGHTY MIGHTY
>   MIGHTY MIGHTY
>   GOOD TA ME
>   oh LAWD
>   MASSA
>   BEEN MY DOCTA
>   IN DA SICKROOM
>   HE BEEN MY LAWYA
>   IN DA COURT –
> HAMMET: he gon'.
> IZZIE MAE: that was a close one.

This is fun. But mistakes routine to fantasy are repeated throughout the play: characters stammer and gasp in disbelief at the time travel business, which the audience accepts without question. And the play comes unhinged at times: when Ron's time-traveling bed lands on a plantation owner, it ignites an incongruous song-and-dance number by jubilant slaves. Some might consider this bravura theater, but I'm not impressed. When you play tennis without a net, you're more likely to execute some brilliant shots – but who wants to watch?

Still, O'Hara's efforts show youthful exuberance and intellectual balance. He concludes with the lesson that slaves and slaveholders – and their descendants – are so intertwined genetically that mistreatment of one group equates to mistreatment of both.

The legacy of slavery also haunts Horton Foote's new play, *The Last of the Thorntons* (Overlook, 2000), set some thirty years ago in a Texas nursing home where Alberta Thornton has been institutionalized for "nervousness." When the play opens, the incorrigible Alberta is misbehaving, to the consternation of the staff. She sits in her room naked, which is preferable to the alternative: walking the halls naked.

Though only sixty years old, Alberta suffers from an Alzheimer's-like condition. More than anything, she wants to go home, but she hasn't got one. She regularly asks Clarabelle, an exasperated employee, to forgive her for slavery (the entire institution). But this is 1970, and Clarabelle – like her parents and grandparents before her – was born into freedom and has no absolution to offer her guilt-ridden charge.

Alberta's obsession stems from a chance encounter with John Ramsey, the descendant of slaves emancipated from the Thornton family's plantation. The young man decreed to Alberta – earnestly or facetiously, it's not clear – that her family lives under a curse, and he instructed her to ask forgiveness of every colored person she meets so that God's punishment on the family might be lifted. And now? "[E]very time I see a colored person I ask them for forgiveness," Alberta reports, "and sometimes they grant it and sometimes they don't, but I always feel better for asking."

Foote's play arrives amid discussion of government restitution to the surviving descendents of chattel slavery, and it addresses the broad, everlooming notion of forgiveness which, along with redemption, forms the foundation of the Christian faith. But the wronged in this case are long dead, and the most egregiously wronged left no progeny. Such is the legacy of a moral calamity of monumental scale: forgiveness and restitution do not pertain.

But I misrepresent Foote's work if I suggest these larger themes are engaged explicitly. *The Last of the Thorntons* offers in dramatic form the subtle inferences and smooth surfaces of a Peter Taylor short story. Any impulse to slight Foote's work for inertness of plot is best left unvoiced, for the author has a trump card: a whopping talent. In his dialogue, Foote attains the clarity and resonance of a great dramatist. Southern dialects can sound to my Midwestern ears like a silly affectation, a lot of hooey: everything Sister this and Papa-Daddy that. But for Foote, these are the materials with which to construct a deeply affecting drama.

The residents of the nursing home speak with the blunt directness of children. With no preparation or segue they address the very core of their dilemma. ("I've got no home anymore.") And elderly Texans have a way of disguising the mechanics of exposition or making it so naked no one much minds. "I was the first white woman born in Harrison," Alberta boasts. "No, you weren't, honey," Miss Fannie Mae Gosset corrects. "That was Mrs. Gallahow. And she's been dead seventy years. You probably don't remember her, darling. But I do. She drove a buggy to town every day."

"Almost everyone's dead I know," babbles Lewis Bowen, age eighty-five. "My mama, Edith, my baby brother. Of course he died when he was ten. Lockjaw. Stepped on a rusty nail. Almost killed Mama."

All is revealed in this crowd. The nursing home is a repository for chatty seniors with no family, just distant kin who rarely visit. ("Well, everybody is so busy these days.") Morbidity, loneliness, desertion, and sadness set the mood, complicated by widespread depression and illness. The characters have no immediate experiences anymore. They make do with memories and tales of murders, epidemics, suicides and wars, wasted fortunes and prison sentences handed down to criminals who have long since passed on. Fannie Mae, a spry seventy-eight-year-old who maintains her own residence but delivers medicine to the home, relates the inevitable change:

> I never sleep the whole night through, rain or not. Before Sitter May, who was my best friend since girlhood, died, when I couldn't sleep I'd get out of bed, put on my clothes, and go quietly out of the house so as not to wake Mama and Bubber, and cross the street to Sitter May's house, who didn't sleep any more than I did, and I'd rap on her window. I didn't have to say a word, just rap, because I knew she'd know who it was, and sure enough out she'd come tiptoeing so as not to wake the rest of her family, and we'd get in my car and ride around to see what was going on until we got sleepy. Now Sitter's dead and I don't like to ride by myself, so Bubber gave me a little portable radio for Christmas that I keep by my bed, and now when I can't sleep, I turn on the radio and listen to people talk.

Perhaps it is understandable that Alberta Thornton clings to the ghosts of her family's slaveholding past. In the face of automated detachment and isolation, evidence of familiar cruelty and the accompanying guilt may serve as comfort, as proof of human contact.

The acceleration of loss at play's end is debilitating, but Alberta's final soliloquy offers no further revelation. Perhaps this is a deliberate decision by the playwright to make more stark Alberta's bleak predicament. Her rambling will not deepen the drama or redeem her fate. She has lost her family, she seeks forgiveness of strangers, she is the last of the Thorntons – and that is all she is.

"Tell us everything," a television reporter instructs a confused Michael Majesky in Don DeLillo's media satire *Valparaiso* (Simon and Schuster, 2000). "Be selective." Journalistic vultures converge after Michael misreads the travel itinerary on a routine business trip, bypassing Valparaiso, Indiana, for Valparaiso, Florida, and continuing on – why not? – to Valparaiso, Chile. The play examines the intrusiveness of a news-obsessed culture that shuns legitimate information and instead inflates a small personal anecdote – an appropriate source of embarrassment among colleagues and friends – into a sustained media event. "Speak. Tell us, Michael," a journalist implores. "We deeply need to know." Coverage expands to include Michael's rocky relationship with his wife Livia, the details of their lovemaking, her dedication to aerobic exercise, her latest pregnancy (by another man), and the couple's teenaged son Andy, whom Michael once nearly killed in a drunken driving accident. Every crevice of Michael's personal life is explored, with his consent. "I accept that," he thoughtfully concedes. "I understand the need for that."

The initial travel mishap, suggested by actual media reports of a man who boarded a flight to Auckland, New Zealand, in lieu of Oakland, California, proves to be a popular and profitable mistake for Michael, though he is subject to considerable harping by the press. ("Say something interesting." "A little faster." "Use the present tense, please.") "A hundred and forty interviews in four and a half days in three and a half cities," Livia reports. "I don't think he's capable of saying one more word until he's had a few hours' sleep."

But with a minimum of cajoling, Michael pushes on, conducting a motivational speaking tour and attending autograph shows on weekends. Finally, a documentary filmmaker suggests shooting a feature-length film of Michael sitting for interviews before competing camera crews, and the phenomenon becomes fully self-referential.

The self-awareness of the participants is of special significance to DeLillo: our culture is sliding into hyperbanality, he suggests, and we all know it yet do nothing about it. "I've come into a stranger's home to do the most superficial sort of dimwit interview," confesses one journalist. "This is the nature of my assignment."

"You invented the legend of Valparaiso," asserts a talk-show host who doesn't accept Michael's mistake at face value. "At some desperate level you surely knew." And under cross-examination Michael admits: "We landed in Santiago. And they convinced me. Airline officials. To go on to Valparaiso. To make the mistake complete. For the human interest."

DeLillo's material resonates for the same reason Peter Weir's 1998 film *The Truman Show* did not. Jim Carrey's Truman was unaware – the innocent victim of a cruel media stunt. But everyone participates knowingly in television culture. From "reality programming" and human interest features to spontaneous diplomatic breakthroughs, everything is scripted, fabricated, or at the very least framed to appear improvised in a predetermined way.

What *Valparaiso* shares with *The Truman Show* is a crushing condescension toward the mass of viewers, with their bone china, their stationary bikes, their osteoporosis. (This is to some extent inevitable, but does Livia need to identify herself as "a part-time unpublished poet"?) More damaging is the play's language. For some of our most respected authors, serious drama – much more than serious fiction – must be incongruous, off-putting, and in violation of its own internal logic.

> INTERVIEWER: Can I ask you? For my own human interest.
> MICHAEL: How my life.
> INTERVIEWER: Yes.
> MICHAEL: Has taken on a luminous quality.
> INTERVIEWER: Yes.
> MICHAEL: A clarity and depth. How I see the precise whiteness of the keys you've been stroking. The egg-whitely nuance. How I see your hand in its particular tonal glow.
> INTERVIEWER: What color?
> MICHAEL: Flesh color.

INTERVIEWER: My God. What else?
MICHAEL: How swingingly my dick comports itself in and out of my pants. What else. How this and how that. How here and how there.

What distinctions can be drawn between good faux-Pinter dialogue and lousy faux-Pinter dialogue? It doesn't much matter: once the lack of dramatic vigor in such passages is apparent, enthusiasm for the piece evaporates.

Elsewhere in *Valparaiso*, DeLillo's dialogue betrays the influence of Christopher Durang, whose comedy *Betty's Summer Vacation* addresses similar themes, with similarly mixed results.

MICHAEL: Are you involved with someone?
INTERVIEWER: I don't like that word.
MICHAEL: Are you having a relationship?
INTERVIEWER: I hate that word. Please. I hate all the words in that sentence.

These lines could have been lifted directly from Durang's early comedy *Beyond Therapy*. Brazenly self-conscious and discontented characters and their vaguely inhuman dialogue are funny when Durang uses them to parody pretentious playwriting. But DeLillo's work is in earnest, and it shows.

[2001]

Edward Albee: The Contrarian Messiah

At the Christlike age of 30, Edward Albee emerged from obscurity as the savoir of American theater by penning his one-act play *The Zoo Story*. Unprecedented notoriety followed the success of *Who's Afraid of Virginia Woolf?* in 1962. Still in his mid-30s, Albee was crucified by the New York critics over his second original full-length play, *Tiny Alice*. The playwright's reputation languished for three decades, but unlike Eugene O'Neill, whose final triumph was posthumous, or Tennessee Williams, who lost and never regained his footing as an artist, Albee witnessed his own second coming in 1994, heralded by the laudatory critical reception to *Three Tall Women*.

Mel Gussow, longtime theater critic for *The New York Times*, emphasizes the ultimately ascendant arc of this playwright's career throughout *Edward Albee: A Singular Journey* (Simon and Schuster, 1999). This is a friendly biography – Gussow has followed Albee's career and socialized with the playwright since the early 1960s. By focusing on Albee's ultimate rejuvenation, Gussow justifies the polite, even protective stance he takes toward Albee's entire oeuvre, which for a time comprised a string of critically drubbed Broadway failures: *All Over*, *Seascape*, *The Lady from Dubuque*, *The Man Who Had Three Arms*. Of Albee's return to critical glory, Gussow writes, "Suddenly, people who had disparaged him in the last decade or more, who thought he was bankrupt as a playwright, were surrounding him with adulation." The implication is that the years of public neglect and critical disfavor were unwarranted, yet without the late success of *Three Tall Women* it would have been exceedingly difficult to make that claim.

Gussow acknowledges the elements of Christian allegory in the playwright's biography, noting repeatedly that Albee was greatly disturbed as a young child upon first hearing the crucifixion story. There is something about the self-willed martyrdom of Jesus Christ that has long fascinated if not obsessed the playwright, Gussow notes. That fascination manifested itself in the young Albee's refusal to engage his studies at Lawrenceville Academy, from which he was expelled, and later at Trinity College, which he was also asked to leave. These minor rebellions were designed to irritate his wealthy adoptive parents and culminated in a complete break with his family at age twenty. The decision to part was Albee's, yet the playwright traces in it echoes of an earlier abandonment by his biological parents. This shift in responsibility finds a parallel in Albee's art: George and Martha kill off their imaginary son just prior to his twenty-first birthday in *Who's Afraid of Virginia Woolf?*

The theme of self-martyrdom is the key to understanding Albee's career. Following his initial rocket-like ascent, Albee was in the enviable position of producing plays "without undue concern about what the public and critical reception might be." There's the rub. Prosperous and acclaimed, Albee set out to please no one but himself, and succeeded. "I always felt he had ascended up to his cerebral cortex for protection after *Virginia Woolf*," Glyn O'Malley, Albee's assistant director, tells Gussow. The composer William Flanagan – Albee's former beau –

expressed concern early on that Albee was indulging in "a reactive, perverse, masochistic high-browism." And Guy Flatley, writing in *The New York Times*, summed up the consensus of the professional critics by dismissing *Tiny Alice* and subsequent works as "inscrutable puzzles, or painful put-ons."

"I write for me," Albee told an interviewer in 1963. "For the audience of me. If other people come along for the ride then it's great." But when other people didn't come along for the ride, Albee lashed out, berating the critics for their stupidity and ridiculing the public for its laziness. Gussow includes a series of anecdotes about esteemed actors – Jessica Tandy, Maureen Stapleton, John Gielgud, Ingrid Bergman – who declined parts in Albee projects or trudged through them with little understanding of or appreciation for the writing. Part of the problem may have been the playwright's intellect and his refusal to pander, but these were not novice performers lacking theater savvy. Something was clearly amiss.

It's possible Albee chose the form, style, and content of his plays with no regard for the audience, but it's also possible he regarded audience members too closely and set out deliberately to displease them, like a school boy cutting classes to spite his parents. In defense of his general brattiness as a youth, Albee has commented, "I think that any kid who has any intelligence, any individuality, has a responsibility to rebel against everything." *Everything?* "Rebellion turns into questioning. I question everything." Just months after *Who's Afraid of Virginia Woolf?* secured his position in the theater world, Albee announced he was working on a new play, an early version of *The Lady from Dubuque*. "I think it's going to be – I hope it will be – just about unbearable," he commented. From Albee, that's a promise.

Gussow walks a fine line defending each Albee work while acknowledging the slump in Albee's career and citing its source: the author himself. "*Tiny Alice* opened the door to self-indulgence, and the critical reception encouraged Albee to be stubbornly defensive. At various other points in his career, he succumbed to what might be called the *Tiny Alice* syndrome." The themes Albee deliberated on – reality versus illusion, worlds within worlds, boxes within boxes – yielded undramatic material that, when executed with less than Borgesian ingenuity, failed to make the leap from banality to profundity. Compounding the problem was Albee's insistence that every project, including the "anti-play" *Box/Mao/Box*, receive full Broadway treatment. Experimental works that might have been more politely received in a smaller venue baffled suburbanites and tourists out for an evening of entertainment, which only exacerbated Albee's contempt for the public – "a most unworthy audience." For ten years following the failure of *The Man Who Had Three Arms*, Albee staged no new works in New York City, in part because of his insistence on Broadway productions that were no longer feasible. He finally relented in 1994, with the successful Off-Broadway staging of *Three Tall Women*.

"Experimental" is an accolade usually reserved for works that take formal risks to no good effect. It's the booby prize for failed innovation. Few would categorize *Three Tall Women* an experimental work because, although it is technically innovative, it is an aesthetic triumph. As was widely noted upon its sensational premiere, *Who's Afraid of Virginia Woolf?* is a flawed work. The author's imperative that we abandon our illusions – contradicting O'Neill's endorsement of pipe dreams – isn't very compelling: it's a simplistic case refuting a simplistic case. And George and Martha's implausible collaboration in self-delusion – an imaginary son – makes the plot creak on its literal level. But the play does send the audience on an exhaustive emotional ride and, almost as neatly as *Catch-22*, its title has entered the general vocabulary to denote a previously unlabeled phenomenon: a couple who torture vulnerable acquaintances with stagy bickering.

In contrast, the success of *Three Tall Women* as a literary work is unqualified – Gussow is right to focus on it throughout his biography. In fact, Gussow's book is a compendium of sound decisions. He surveys Albee's juvenilia and apprentice works quickly and painlessly. He debunks the myth that, because Albee was produced first in Germany, New York theater professionals must have been too obtuse to recognize his talent. (*The Zoo Story*, in fact, reached the Off-Broadway stage with unusual speed for a one-act play by a first-time author.) Gussow has admiration and enthusiasm for his subject, but he does not debase the playwright or playwrights in general with an explicit Ranking of the Greats. And he examines the artist's fallow period honestly: he suggests Albee's twenty-year bout of heavy drinking, including a ten-year bout of debilitating drinking (from 1967 to 1977), sapped Albee of creative power and left him an arrogant, mean drunk.

"What he had lost (or never had) in his childhood," Gussow writes, "he has been seeking as an adult, and as an artist." The same could be said of any author, but childhood is of paramount concern to an Albee biographer. Albee's unhappy adoption by nouveau riche parents left him with a nagging sense of transience. (They gave him "all the things money could buy.") As an artist, he was confused about where his talent came from. Albee's family members appear in his plays: the grotesques in *The Sandbox* and *The American Dream*, the declaiming WASPs in *A Delicate Balance*, and of course the elderly mother – the anti-muse – at the center of *Three Tall Women*. In fact, Albee's adoption and family drama are central obsessions in his work. "They bought me," the playwright laments, and he seems unable to shake that thought.

Albee has never kept a journal and has rarely corresponded. To reconstruct Albee's biography, Gussow relies on the playwright's memories, his plays, published interviews, and the comments of friends and colleagues, who attest to Albee's influence on a generation of playwrights. It may be difficult now to fully appreciate the affect Albee had on New York theater in the early 1960s – how he freed the stage in terms of language, form, and content for Sam Shepard, Lanford Wilson, David Mamet, and others. As John Guare, reflecting on *The Zoo Story*, notes, "Albee spawned an entire generation of park bench plays." Unfortunately, what emerges most memorably from this biography, despite Gussow's best efforts, is not Albee's early influence or his late success, but the fact that Albee suffered a decades-long slump in between. Albee long fancied himself a prophet rejected by his own people: his biological parents, the Larchmont couple who adopted him, the theater-going public. But, in fact, the latter two rejections were the result of maneuverings by the playwright himself – a man who chose to rebel against everything, including his own success and the role God chose for him as the Messiah of Broadway.

[2001]

AUGUST WILSON GROUNDED

When *Seven Guitars* opened on March 28, 1996, at the Walter Kerr Theatre in New York City, it became August Wilson's sixth consecutive commercial success on Broadway in fewer than twelve years. Like Wilson's five previous plays – *Ma Rainey's Black Bottom* (1984), *Fences* (1987), *Joe Turner's Come and Gone* (1988), *The Piano Lesson* (1990), and *Two Trains Running* (1992) – *Seven Guitars* was directed by Lloyd Richards, then head of the Yale Drama School and artistic director of the O'Neill Playwrights Conference, to which Wilson owes his professional rise. And, also like the five previous plays, *Seven Guitars* won critical acclaim and high-profile accolades, including the New York Drama Critics Circle Award. But Wilson chose regional-theater veteran Marion McClinton, not Richards, to direct a rewritten apprentice work, *Jitney*, at the Pittsburgh Public Theatre later that year. McClinton subsequently helmed the play's 2000 New York production as well as the premiere the following year of a new work, *King Hedley II*.

Still in 1996, Wilson delivered an address at the 11th biennial Theatre Communications Group national conference at Princeton University. Published five years later as *The Ground on Which I Stand* (TCG, 2001), the speech ruffled feathers by demanding more equitable funding for African-American regional theaters, which Wilson claimed were almost nonexistent, and by criticizing in extremely scathing language nontraditional or "color-blind" casting, a practice by which African-American actors play characters originally written or performed as white.

Since giving the speech and switching directors, Wilson's commercial clout has ceased its ascent and his critical reputation has suffered, if temporarily. *Jitney* won the author a seventh New York Drama Critics Circle Award, but the reviews were polite rather than enthusiastic, and the play ran Off-Broadway – a financial retreat and an irritant to Wilson. *King Hedley II* had a much rougher time of it. After pre-Broadway stops in Pittsburgh, Seattle, Boston, Los Angeles, and Chicago, the touring production arrived at the Kennedy Center in Washington, D.C., in February 2001 for a final tune-up with star Brian Stokes Mitchell still consulting his script onstage, so extensive were last-minute rewrites after more than a year on the road. The critical reception in New York was predictably mixed, and the Broadway production was a commercial disappointment – a first for the playwright.

The decline in Wilson's fortunes is likely a mere blip in an astonishingly sustained career (arguably overdue in a business characterized by erratic and often arbitrary fluctuations). Still, the unenthusiastic reception to this author's first major play set in nearly contemporary times is worthy of note. As Wilson was nearing completion of a decade-by-decade project chronicling the African-American experience of the twentieth century, he reportedly considered for a time combining the remaining two works, pegged to the first and final decades of the century, thus hastening the project's end. "He is making noises about retiring," observed John Lahr in an April 2001 *New Yorker* magazine profile of the playwright. "[H]e has recently begun to take stock of his life and resolve 'to do something different.'"

The link between Wilson's professional convulsions and his bitter attack on the theater community may be merely coincidental. This is, after all, an author who has made controversial statements in interviews and published essays for some time. His 1996 address, while the most notorious and highly publicized of these, is not unique; the author was not experiencing some sudden expository meltdown at Princeton. Toward his own role in the dramatic process, Wilson frequently shows exemplary wisdom, generosity, and common sense. "The playwright has a responsibility to the audience," he explained in a 1987 interview. "I'm asking people to hire a babysitter, get dressed, find the car keys, find a place to park, pay money – more than it costs to go see a movie. When they get there, I should have something to say to them that's worth all their trouble." But on broader matters – economic, political, racial – he has made startling pronouncements that, until 1996 at least, were given a confoundedly respectful hearing. The loopiest of these was his extended exultation for blacks to return to the South, their "ancestral homeland," in order to acquire economic and political clout as a concentrated demographic group. "We should all move tomorrow, while we still can before the government says we can't," he told Richard Pettengill with customary paranoia in 1993. "If five million people were to move to, let's say, Alabama or Georgia, that's five million people that suddenly have to be fed. That means someone's going to have to own supermarkets. That's five million people that need to be housed. Who owns the lumber yards? Just in the process of providing food, clothing and shelter, you create jobs for yourself. Then you begin an economic base. You build houses for five million people, then you take all that money and open you up a bank. Suddenly, we're talking about hundreds of millions of dollars here, just in lumber."

Is it necessary to point out that things don't run that smoothly in the economic sphere? Wilson has cited negative aspects of the mass migration northward of African Americans, and of desegregation in general – fewer black-owned businesses, no black sports leagues, diluted political power, and so on – but he has completely discounted the economic realities and moral imperatives that brought them about. Yet the case Wilson made for an unworkable alternative to our present situation went largely unchallenged in a theater community where cracked ideas on important matters rarely get examined with intellectual rigor. John Lahr delicately summed up Wilson's advocacy for black remigration to the South innocuously, stating: "his very specific anthropological understanding of American history has led him to some hard, politically incorrect opinions."

It would be a mistake, of course, to assume that every gifted storyteller possesses valuable insight into the political and economic problems of his day. And apparently few make that erroneous assumption about Wilson, who has been given a pass when he shoots off at the mouth. This is in part, I believe, because the topics he addresses either lead to shear fantasy, as above, or keep the playwright harmlessly self-absorbed. In his 1990 essay "I Want a Black Director,"

Wilson insisted that the movie version of *Fences* be directed by an African American. ("We have different ideas about style, about language. We have different aesthetics.") This may have cost one director a job – Barry Levinson had reportedly been under consideration by the studio – but repercussions in the industry at large were mild so the response was muted. Moreover, the personal digs Wilson makes at artists who disagree with him more often than not backfire. A case in point: Wilson mocked Eddie Murphy, who was involved for a time on the *Fences* project, for objecting, "I don't want to hire nobody just 'cause they black." The author insisted Murphy misunderstood the cultural nuances of his demands as well as the stakes involved. But our sympathies go immediately to the actor, a successful Hollywood veteran who has no doubt watched helplessly as the quality of his films suffer from studio decisions influenced by nepotism, a casting-couch performance, or other considerations as dubious as Wilson's insistence on a black director. There is no point undermining Wilson, then, because he so effectively undermines himself.

But there have been times, especially more recently, when the playwright has stepped over the line of benign offensiveness and his ideas have become objectionable. For me, the line was crossed most egregiously in "Prescriptions for a Troubled Patient: The Theater," a *New York Times* article from October 31, 1999, in which Wilson was quoted making the assertion that theater is a tool one uses to address the public. "And you can look at it in terms of the First Amendment right to free speech and the constitutional guarantee of that," he stated. "But the lack of access to funding that will allow you to make that speech can be considered a prior restraint." The implications of such a statement are obviously troubling. Since the vast majority of playwrights do not receive financial subsidy, it follows that the government is denying dramatists their constitutional rights *en masse*.

It pains me to see the concept of free speech taken for granted and undermined by artists who resort to opportunistic distortion. Similar objections prompted Robert Brustein, artistic director of the American Repertory Theatre in Boston, to suggest that Wilson was merely stinging from a recent loss at the 1996 Tony Awards when the playwright issued his diatribe at the TCG conference on June 26 of that year. For it was Brustein – in a 1996 *New Republic* article, "Subsidized Separatism," and at a debate with Wilson at New York's Town Hall in 1997 – who finally stood up and refuted one of Wilson's rants. *The Ground on Which I Stand* elicited a formal response from a scion of the theater establishment because, unlike many of Wilson's previous statements, this one addressed the failings of the theater community itself and took specific issue with an essay Brustein wrote criticizing the theater bureaucracy's tendency to reward "diversity" at the expense of talent.

In *The Ground on Which I Stand*, Wilson states: "We cannot share a single value system if that value system consists of the values of white Americans based on their European ancestors. We reject that as Cultural Imperialism. We need a value system that includes our contributions as Africans in America." In short, this pamphlet is a forty-six page rephrasing of novelist Zora Neale Hurston's comment that white people couldn't be trusted to collect the folklore of others. Wilson complains that theaters developing black playwrights are at a financial disadvantage to mainstream institutions that ignore African-American authors or, at best, encourage them to deny their heritage. In arguing his point, Wilson makes one very crucial but nearly inadvertent observation: Brustein's defense of aesthetic criteria "only serves to call into question the tremendous outpouring of plays by white playwrights who benefit from funding."

Indeed, the outcome of *any* funding decision, based on *whatever* criteria, will raise hackles – a point with which Brustein likely would agree. The clique of separatist black theaters Wilson envisions is just one of several imperfect scenarios possible in an artistic milieu that has long since lost its economic viability and independence. What sets Wilson apart from Brustein or anyone else who might draw up competing sets of funding criteria are the nasty, bullying tactics the playwright uses to denigrate unsupportive colleagues, black and white. For example, he divides the black theater community into two camps, deriving from separate traditions. One highly undignified tradition originated when slaves were summoned to the "big house" to entertain the slave owner and his guests. "This tradition has its present-life counterpart in the crossover artists that slant their material for white consumption," Wilson observes. Practitioners of a second tradition confined themselves to private environs, where their art, song, and dance became invested with spiritual significance drawn from African ancestors. "I stand myself and my art squarely on the self-defining ground of the slave quarters," he needlessly informs us.

If many of Wilson's black theater colleagues come off badly here – as complacent house niggers and Uncle Toms – they should count their blessings: his white colleagues get castigated as Simon Legrees. To hire a black actor for a "white" play does not reflect well on the actor's talent or assist him in any way, according to Wilson. Rather, it denies him his own competence, consigning him to the role of mimic. "Our manners, our style, our approach to language, our gestures, and our bodies are not for rent," he fumes. "The history of our bodies – the maimings, the lashings, the lynchings, the body that is capable of inspiring profound rage and pungent cruelty – is not for rent."

An artistic director who gives no consideration to race, I would argue, has little in common with a slave owner who resorts to violence and torture. To compare the two in moral terms, as Wilson does, is worse than unseemly. But it is not out of character for a playwright who objects to desegregation in general because it has denied black-owned establishments a monopoly on their customer base. In this light, the specifics of Wilson's TCG address are not surprising. They are simply the application of his general ideas to the specifics of theater.

Nor is it a surprise that Wilson has a clouded view of theatrical institutions and their relationship to playwrights, especially African Americans. When the art of the slave quarters becomes the object of intense white interest and acclaim, where are you: in the "big house" pleasing the master, or still at home with your integrity intact? This is the dilemma Wilson finds himself in, and which he chooses not to confront. "Does it bother you that your audiences are mostly white?" an interviewer asked in 1999. "I don't think about it," he replied. The recipient of numerous fellowships and grants – Jerome, Bush, Rockefeller, McKnight, Guggenheim – prior to the 1987 Broadway premiere of *Fences*, which grossed $11 million in its first year (a record at the time for a nonmusical production), Wilson can grouse only on behalf of others. "[H]e has become a very rich man," John Lahr has assured us, "and he is only getting richer." Even the disappointing Broadway run of *King Hedley II* seems not to have hurt his pocketbook much, thanks to his clout and the unique joint venture he has entered into which pays him both a writer's and a producer's share of profits. "A Wilson play has a gestation period like no other in the history of American theatre," Lahr noted, referring to the fact that *King Hedley II* played numerous cities prior to its New York run. A lucrative national tour normally serves as the spoils of a Broadway hit, but in Wilson's case, the reception of the New York premiere comes after the fact and is therefore less relevant to the production's overall solvency and profitability.

What remains vexing is the problem of subject matter, and Wilson's need to shape his material as its timeline moves toward the end of the century. *Jitney*, a minor early work, has assumed the 1970s slot in Wilson's cycle of plays; *King Hedley II* is set in 1985; the 1990s play remains to be written. In previous works, set in previous decades, Wilson featured exceptional characters – the blues singer Ma Rainey; Troy Maxson, a baseball great, in *Fences*; another musician, Floyd Barton, in *Seven Guitars* – who were denied the royalties and acclaim their talents merited. But what can Wilson do at century's end, now that the Michael Jordans and Tiger Woods, the Janet Jacksons and August Wilsons of the sports and entertainment worlds enjoy the disproportionate wealth awarded to the top echelon of individual talents? An August Wilson play about a miser counting his gold pieces might be a very interesting work indeed, but I don't see this playwright going that route. For his 1980s play, he chose a violent and in some ways pathetic title character who is neither gifted nor usefully focused in his efforts, but who – like the annoying, untalented hip-hop stars who were emerging at that time – somehow views himself as deserving of success.

I fear Wilson will feel compelled to make similarly unfortunate decisions in his 1990s play. He may himself be experiencing a certain trepidation, which would explain the fleeting plan to combine that work with the '00s play and have done with the cycle. The backdrop to *King Hedley II* was the economic restructuring instituted under Ronald Reagan, now generally acknowledged as necessary and ultimately beneficial to all strata of society, but vilified by the playwright as crisis-inducing and particularly cruel to African Americans. I doubt the tacit endorsement of Reagan's economic policies by Bill Clinton, Al Gore, and other New Democrats in the 1990s, and the subsequent expansion of economic growth to black communities, in fulfillment of Reagan's predictions, have done anything to placate the author or lay the groundwork for a 1990s play that acknowledges these developments. And that's probably just as well. Modern playwrights, as we know, are natural contrarians. Robert Brustein, who wrote *The Theatre of Revolt* in 1964, added more recently, "The greatest modern European artists, like August Wilson himself, have almost invariably been rebels against the existing culture, not its proselytes and flunkies." The irony in this case is that Wilson's critique of the status quo advocates an empowered black citizenry who would draw on the traditions of Africa, where no such contrarian figure is permitted. That is, the artist or intellectual who stands to the side and condemns his own society as ill-conceived and misguided is not a feature of African cultures, whose inhabitants venerate their ancestors and are inclined to accept without resistance the often unjust traditions and arbitrary taboos that are handed down to them. By condemning our economic system as well as a theater community that shines a bright spotlight on his belligerent works, Wilson is advocating his own obsolescence.

[2001]

Middlebrow Annoyances

"I love vaginas. I love women. I do not see them as separate things," states a female character in one of the brief narratives Eve Ensler patched together from interviews with more than two hundred women to form *The Vagina Monologues* (Villard, 1998). In the play's introduction, Ensler describes her own vagina as "my motor, my center, my second heart." And a participant in a workshop on sexual discovery, peering at her vagina for the first time in a handheld mirror, reports: "It made me laugh. It could hide and seek, open and close. It was a mouth. It was the morning. And then it momentarily occurred to me that it was *me*, my vagina: it was who *I* was."

Throughout *The Vagina Monologues*, embarrassing scatological phenomena such as excessive vaginal lubrication and menstruation are examined as portals to female truth. These have male counterparts, of course, also originating at puberty: wet dreams, inopportune erections, premature ejaculation. But parallel male experiences are not considered here. Gendered pairs of words like *vagina* and *penis* cannot be instructively interpolated, the work implies, because the female experience is uniquely traumatic. Ensler says the word vagina 128 times in her one-women show because, she explains, she's not supposed to say it. "I say it because it's an invisible word – a word that stirs up anxiety, awkwardness, contempt, and disgust." The playwright expects audience members to wince at her bravado. But the taboo she is breaking is aesthetic not social; it applies to all self-congratulatory artists who have an inflated sense of their own daring.

"I say 'vagina,'" Ensler continues, "because I have read the statistics, and bad things are happening to women's vaginas everywhere: 500,000 women are raped every year in the United States; 100 million women have been genitally mutilated worldwide; and the list goes on and on. I say 'vagina' because I want these bad things to stop." Kudos to Ensler for attempting to overturn centuries of cultural inertia, but such a Herculean task demands, among other things, a crisp intelligence sorely missing from *The Vagina Monologues*. "I had been performing this piece for over two years," Ensler admits, "when it suddenly occurred to me that there were no pieces about birth. It was a bizarre omission." Indeed, it was. Camille Paglia has spent the past decade expounding on the sublime power of female reproduction, classifying ostentatious cultural artifacts as futile attempts by men to compensate for a missing uterus. Ensler, oblivious, still finds herself in need of instruction on such elementary matters as reclaiming the nominally pejorative word *cunt*.

Emily Mann, Anna Deavere Smith and, more recently, Marc Wolf have developed compelling theatrical works using an interview technique similar to Ensler's. And some of the respondents in *The Vagina Monologues* are amusing and insightful people. But the fact that the narratives in Ensler's play are composites undercuts the genre's greatest strength: its documentary immediacy. Worse, the subject matter seems to have relieved the playwright of any obligation to artistic discipline.

In short, Ensler shows no real command of her material. That nine interviewed women experience their first orgasms at vagina-gazing seminars (which include a unit on masturbation) sets an adolescent tone the author never addresses. (In stark contrast, comedian Denis Leary managed to sum up the appeal of Robert Bly's *Iron John* movement in two words: circle jerk.) Ensler hopes one day to feel no shame or guilt when saying the word vagina. But if clinical, straight talk is what she's after, her methods are counterproductive. Ensler forces all 200-plus women she interviews to participate in the sort of word-association exercises that distance women from their bodies and yield misleading, cutesy answers. "If your vagina got dressed, what would it wear?" Ensler asks. "If your vagina could talk, what would it say?"

In her political drama *An American Daughter* (Harcourt Brace, 1998), Wendy Wasserstein considers Middle America's hostility toward successful women and the media's culpability in fomenting that hostility. The failed nominations of Zoe Baird and Kimba Wood for Attorney General in 1993 serve as catalysts for what Wasserstein calls "a fractured fairy tale depicting both a social and a political dilemma for contemporary professional women."

Dr. Lyssa Dent Hughes, the play's 42-year-old title character, seems a safe nominee for Surgeon General: she's a dedicated health care professional whose father serves in the Senate, though for the opposition party. With her political bases covered, Lyssa permits reporter Timber Tucker to film her in a segment for a fluffy news program. "This is going to make really boring television," Lyssa's best friend warns. "Judith," Lyssa responds with one eye firmly on the audience, "if I have to explain to Timber Tucker over pancakes that gun control is really a health issue, it's worth it to me. And if he wants to watch me pick up my kids from soccer practice so every woman in this country is assured reproductive freedom, it's also worth it to me. And I happen to know its worth it to you too."

But Lyssa's husband, Walter, lets slip on camera that his wife once ignored – or possibly misplaced – a jury summons. The press seizes on the information with carnival-like glee, and the electorate is outraged – at *Lyssa*. She schedules a second television appearance to act chastened and thereby salvage her appointment, but it too goes haywire. Coached to act docile and apologetic, Lyssa instead turns combative in the play's best-written scene. "There's nothing quite so satisfying as erasing the professional competency of a woman, is there?" she demands theatrically when challenged about her fitness for public service. Her outburst does not precisely address the nomination difficulties faced by Baird, Wood, Lani Guinier, and others early in the first Clinton administration, but it may accurately reflect the nominees' own view of events, which is all that matters here. In a final act of defiance, Lyssa withdraws her name from consideration.

Prior to that well-modulated dénouement, however, Wasserstein loads the drama with some of the least subtle dialogue I have encountered in a professionally produced play, particularly when driving home the point that Lyssa is a morally unimpeachable nominee. "My daughter was always a do-gooder," Senator Alan Hughes reports. "She was a candy striper in the hospital, she was on the

Indian reservation for her college vacations, she was always busy starting rape centers, birthing centers, and let's-get-together-and-help-women centers. My daughter Lyssa believes that every day it's time to smile on your sister." This PR plug is delivered not to Timber Tucker in front of the cameras but, rather, to family and friends once the reporter has left the room.

Everyone in the play is assigned a simplistic political label, which the audience is notified of prior to or upon the character's initial entrance. Even persons who never appear on stage are so identified for no reason. Describing a Harvard professor who has turned absurdly violent, Lyssa's husband informs us, "He's a brilliant guy. Very respected sociologist. Left wing." Lyssa, of course, is left wing, while a family friend, Morrow McCarthy, is right wing, as his name not so quietly suggests. When Walter invites Morrow to the televised brunch, Lyssa curses.

> WALTER: What's the matter?
> LYSSA: Do you really want Morrow to be here with that reporter?
> WALTER: Why not? Because he's gay?
> LYSSA: Walter, don't be ridiculous. I love Morrow, but his new antiabortion stand is not exactly how I want to represent myself.
> WALTER: It's not new. He's always had his faith.
> LYSSA: I just wish he'd find a boyfriend and leave women's reproductive rights alone.

This discussion recommences just as baldly once Morrow and Quincy Quince, a former student of Walter's, arrive for brunch.

> MORROW: Lyssa, we've been having a heated debate over the role of religion and sex in a secular society.
> QUINCY: Senator, how much do your religious beliefs account for your antichoice position on abortion?
> ALAN: Miss Quince – I love saying your name, Miss Quince – I like to think that my beliefs account for an open dialogue.
> LYSSA: Dad, your beliefs on this subject are untenable. How can you be so adamant about individual rights, and deny the most personal right, when and if to have a child?
> MORROW: All life, physical or intellectual, begins at conception.

Wasserstein seems to have watched a lot of roundtable discussion shows on Sunday morning television. Her political-insider characters make conveniently expository quips that sound like "spontaneous" journalistic give-and-take. These are followed by appeals for affirmation like "Am I right, Senator?" and "Aren't I right, Walter?" until Judith, speaking on behalf of us all, finally barks, "I'm not interested in your sound bites."

Pauline Kael once dismissed a forgettable Goldie Hawn-Burt Reynolds film as a "Velveeta comedy." For three-quarters of its duration, Wasserstein's foray into political drama invites a similarly wilting dismissal. Making matters worse, the author is smug and self-important in defense of her play, both in interviews and the preface to the printed script. "This play, more than my others, is a play of ideas," she explains. "Pat Collins, the noblest of lighting designers, would sidle up to me during tech rehearsals and whisper, 'No one else is saying this!'"

Throughout her career, Wendy Wasserstein has shown not the slightest awareness of her own upper-middle-class sense of entitlement – the very sin attributed to Baird and Wood. Indeed, the playwright likens the lambasting she received upon the play's Broadway opening to Lyssa's mistreatment by media and the *hoi polloi*. Male critics and audience members not favorably disposed to her play *just don't get it*.

Diana Son's breakthrough drama, *Stop Kiss* (Overlook, 1999), opens with a private karaoke scene familiar from innumerable Hollywood movies. One of the two young female leads closes the blinds, locks the door, and places tape over the peep hole in order to lip synch a pop song unseen. This episode alludes to our fear of detection by the outside world – our need to hide our true selves and our most honest behavior. But we've seen it too many times before: the corny professionalism and faux polish, the sheepishness upon discovery. Rather than endear the character to us, the karaoke performance merely signals we are in the hands of a playwright who resorts to stock devices.

Commissioned by Playwrights Horizons and workshopped at The Playwrights Center in Minneapolis, *Stop Kiss* premiered back in New York at The Joseph Papp Public Theater. This is an impressive pedigree for what is essentially a cloying Manhattan love story. Callie meets Sara, a newly arrived schoolteacher, and they tentatively maneuver their friendship toward romance. Their first attempt at a kiss, however, is interrupted by a lesbophilic maniac who, denied the opportunity to observe, bashes Sara into a coma.

That violent incident gives the work its "high concept." It also gives Son a reason to tell half the play in flashbacks. The structure builds tension as we head inevitably toward a scene whose aftermath we have already witnessed. It also takes the melodramatic edge off the plot, as does the playwright's decision to push Sara into baiting her attacker. We are told Sara admires a brave eight-year-old student who talks back to mouthy crackheads. "The best thing to do is walk on by," Callie advises prophetically. But Sara ignores the advice, thus sealing her fate.

Its effective structure aside, the play is dominated by middlebrow annoyances. In scene nine, for example, the author attempts to milk laughs from the fact that Callie is an incompetent cook who burns dinner. And Sara's devotion to teaching public schoolchildren in New York City is oversold and sentimental. I've refrained till now from mentioning that Son is a staff writer for the NBC drama series *The West Wing*, which should come as no surprise.

The playwright's handling of the story's homosexual subtext struck me as very odd. I'm not referring to the fact that the two heretofore heterosexual main characters suffer a violent rebuke the very first time they kiss, though that's an oddity in itself. I was more confused by the investigative technique of Detective Cole, the NYPD official assigned to the case. In scene two, he asks Callie what bar the women stopped at prior to the beating (Callie lies to cover her lesbian tracks), who bought the drinks, and if the bartender was short and stocky or tall and skinny. After grilling the evasive Callie for some time, hoping to trip her up and expose her errant sexuality, he finally asks for a description of their attacker.

In scene four, Cole is equally suspicious of Mrs. Winsley, the Greenwich Village resident who called 911 the night of the attack, though Mrs. Winsley has evaded none of his questions. Cole later insinuates that Mrs. Winsley's husband is gay. None of this bears on the case or the veracity of Mrs. Winsley's testimony – *what is going on here?* I get the feeling a few ill-conceived plot elements – like making Detective Cole a raving homophobe – were considered and dropped, or semi-dropped, while Son workshopped and revised the script.

Midway through the play, Peter flies in from St. Louis to visit his comatose ex-girlfriend. The scene between Peter and his rival, Callie, in the hospital waiting room elicits an unexpected burst of honesty from the playwright and raises the surprisingly pertinent subject of natural selection.

> PETER: Why couldn't you protect her?
> CALLIE: He was big, he was stronger – I tried –
> PETER: How big.
> CALLIE: I *tried.*
> PETER: Bigger than me?
>   *Callie turns away from him.*
> PETER: Could I have –
>   *He turns her back.*
> PETER: Hey, was he bigger than me?
> CALLIE: No!
>   *Peter steps back.*
> PETER: Why was she protecting you?

But the story concludes with a bit of hokum. Rather than return to St. Louis for extensive physical therapy, the brain-damaged Sara, we are expected to believe, prefers to remain in New York City. Her weeks-old friendship with Callie, which may develop into a lasting love affair but – let's be realistic – probably will not, trumps a supportive network of family, friends, and a lover of seven years. I don't believe it for a second.

Woody Allen's character in *Annie Hall,* Alvy Singer, distorts memories of his youth, misplacing his childhood home directly under the roller coaster at Coney Island. In Suzan-Lori Parks' new play, *In the Blood* (Dramatists Play Service, 2000), the illiterate lead character – Hester, La Negrita – resides with similar absurdity under a graffiti-strewn bridge with her five impoverished children. Their predicament is attributable not to a narrator's bitter nostalgia but to the hypocrisy of agencies charged with assisting the poor and – equally important – to Hester's own stubborn attachment to indigence. "We at Welfare are at the end of our rope with you, Hester," scolds a female bureaucrat identified in the script simply as Welfare, who extorts a shoulder rub from her client.

> WELFARE: We build bridges you burn them. We sew safety nets, rub harder, good strong safety nets and you slip through the weave.
> HESTER: We was getting by all right, then I dunno, I been tired lately. Like something in me broke.

In Hester's defense, every adult character in the play exploits her sexually, financially, or – most often – both. Representing the religious community, the medical community, the government, and the institutions of friendship and marriage, the cast of characters relentlessly dumps on Hester, making it impossible for her to escape her material and emotional impoverishment. "As a writer my job is to write good plays," Parks has declared; "it's also to defend dramatic literature against becoming 'Theatre of Schmaltz.'" Yet Parks flirts with schmaltzy dramatic effects throughout *In the Blood*. Hester's despair predates her present misery, but it is compounded by relentless mistreatment at the hands of others. This mentally sound and resourceful woman will never succeed at anything.

"Black presence on stage is more than a sign or messenger of some political point," Parks once asserted. "The Klan does not always have to be outside the door for Black people to have lives worthy of dramatic literature." But if not the Klan, then the "Higher Ups" assault Hester via their emissaries. The character called Doctor reports on the pressure he is under to corral wayward women and sterilize them. "The Higher Ups are breathing down my back, Hester. They want answers! They want results! Solutions! Solutions! Solutions! That's what they want."

"Some people think I'm an issue-oriented writer," Parks told Kathy Sova in a March 2000 interview, "but I've never said to myself, 'I'm going to write about such-and-such an issue' – that would make for incredibly boring writing, at least to my taste." Still, the "issue" here – the Clinton-Gingrich welfare reform of the mid-90s – is harshly spotlighted. "I would want to be paid a living wage," the Amiga Gringa, Hester's indigent friend, tells her, using the media vernacular of the moment. What prevents the piece from becoming the sort of unambitious work of political art that Parks is bored by is, first, the author's craft and talent, which are considerable, and, second, the fact that Hester is inert.

> HESTER: My lifes my own fault. I know that. But the world dont help, Maam.
> WELFARE: The world is not here to help us, Hester. The world is simply here. We must help ourselves.

How is one to read that passage? Welfare's statement is true, as far as it goes. But this is probably the last thing a caseworker should be telling a client struggling to feed five children residing under a bridge. Still, Hester is clearly in need of what 12-step groups and conservative pundits call "tough love," for the sake of her children if nothing else. Hester even denies them a hot meal from a shelter because the staff there "hassle" her. This uncompromising attitude, exacerbated by additional bad breaks, leads to the play's violent and utterly convincing climax.

In her 1995 essay "An Equation for Black People Onstage," Parks called for a new bullshit-free dramatic equation that features an x factor, "where x is the realm of situations showing African-Americans in states other than the Oppressed by/Obsessed with 'Whitey' state." *In the Blood* reads at times like a satire of Oppressed-by-Whitey drama. Yet Parks plays it straight. Luckily, the author's ambivalence saves the play: her black female lead suffers but also contributes mightily to her own tragic end.

[2001]

Neil Simon on Autopilot

Neil Simon's second volume of memoirs, *The Play Goes On* (Simon and Schuster, 1999), is handicapped from the start. The death of Simon's beloved first wife, Joan, casts a pall over this entire book, making subsequent relationships insignificant and transient by comparison to their idealized union. Simon's second marriage was passed in an amnesic blur of workaholic avoidance. And Simon's third wife insisted on a prenuptial agreement forbidding the author to report personal details of their relationship. This is not a promising scenario for a memoir. Because the years covered in *The Play Goes On* – 1973 to 1998 – are of considerable importance to the development of Simon's craft, one would hope this volume could at least provide insight into the artistic growth of America's most popular playwright. Unfortunately, this is rarely the case.

In 1973, the newly widowed Simon went to work on *The Good Doctor*, a stage adaptation of several Chekhov stories, just to occupy his time and get himself through the crisis of losing a wife. It was a strategy on which he relied throughout the subsequent decade, though it is unclear when the flurry of writing ceased being a response to Joan Simon's death and became instead a device to avoid dealing with his failing second marriage to actress Marsha Mason. Simon began to write, in his own words, "continuously, compulsively, relentlessly." He tells us: "I was writing shows and screenplays with such regularity that I have no memory of exactly when I wrote them, and how, because they were usually squeezed in between two other projects with which I was deeply involved." And: "I was working, I suppose, on automatic control, and like a well-made toaster, I was popping out crusty English muffins that everyone seemed to enjoy." Among the scripts Simon produced during those years were the screenplay to *The Goodbye Girl* and the play *Chapter Two*, both featuring Mason. The marriage, however, could not be salvaged. When Simon announced he was flying to Connecticut to rehearse his play *Actors and Actresses* rather than remain in California to work on their marriage, Mason moved out. "[F]or the first time in years," Simon remembers, "I had no desire to write a single word."

The author has little recollection of those Connecticut rehearsals, coming as they did in the midst of a personal crisis. The same could be said of a number of his other theater projects, and it pretty well sums up the shortcomings of this book. We count on a memoirist to remember, after all. In particular, we expect a successful playwright to relate his theater experiences, as Simon did in his previous book, *Rewrites*. This second volume brings to mind those stock Hollywood film sequences suggesting the passage of time: we're shown a close-up of hands typing frenetically, and a kaleidoscopic montage of twirling theater marquees. But the book is heavy on segue, and light on story.

The Play Goes On is not entirely bereft of anecdotes or show business lore. Simon informs us: he turned down Warren Beatty's request to write the screenplay for *Heaven Can Wait*; the hilarious *Richard III* scenes in *The Goodbye Girl* were inspired by a lamentable Lincoln Center production of the Shakespeare play starring Michael Moriarty and Marsha Mason; Robert De Niro was originally (mis)cast in the Richard Dreyfuss role in the same film; and Simon doctored the script of *A Chorus Line*, goosing it with jokes just prior to the musical's opening. But these are the exceptions. There is little here to rival the fascinating accounts in *Rewrites* of Simon and director Mike Nichols as they completely overhaul *The Odd Couple* during its out-of-town run, or the headaches associated with shepherding *Plaza Suite* from its Boston tryouts to Broadway, with the egos of George C. Scott and Maureen Stapleton in tow. In *Rewrites*, Simon recounted his theater experiences; in this second volume, he summarizes them. "Our twelve-character cast were simply wonderful and too numerous to list all their names here," Simon concludes about his farce *Rumors*. The production of *Jake's Women* gets boiled down to: "Thanks to Alan Alda's brilliant and demanding performance as Jake, the play had a successful run on Broadway and then again in Los Angeles."

It's not that the casts of his plays became less notable. *The Good Doctor*, for example, featured Christopher Plummer, Frances Sternhagen, Rene Auberjonois, and Marsha Mason, and *Lost in Yonkers* starred Irene Worth, Mercedes Reuhl, and Kevin Spacey. We're told details of Marsha Mason's audition for *The Good Doctor* because it has repercussions for the author's private life, and Simon transcribes the uncomfortable interview with Irene Worth prior to signing her to the cast of *Lost in Yonkers*. But little is said of the rehearsal process, cast member rivalries, or rewrites except for additions made to showcase the talents of the author's wife. Is it possible that, as he matured as a writer, Simon no longer substantially reshaped his material during rehearsals and out-of-town tryouts? If so, that is a significant development that should be stated explicitly, not implied by the author's silence.

There is an ominous passage in the second half of *The Play Goes On*: the very afternoon Simon marries his third wife, Diane Lander, he gets the urge to retreat to this office and write for a few hours. But for whatever reason, this marriage, which also fails – twice – does not send the author into the same mindless writing frenzy as before. In fact, these years produce Simon's most carefully considered work: the autobiographical trilogy comprising *Brighton Beach Memoirs*, *Biloxi Blues*, and *Broadway Bound*, plus *Lost in Yonkers*. Simon does not consider if his manic productivity may have been necessary to flush out the residue from previous, less serious efforts, but that may be the inference of those who find his earlier comedies clogged with sentimentality. The success of these four plays was especially satisfying to Simon, since they followed a string of commercial failures and the Shubert production organization passed on *Brighton Beach Memoirs*, deeming it uncommercial. That play ran four years on Broadway, revived Simon's career, and sent him into new territory which he perfected in *Lost in Yonkers*.

Simon's longevity in theater means he has witnessed innumerable changes in the business, many of them worrisome. "Twenty-five years ago," he writes, "when the New York theater had an abundance of new plays, an actor could go to two or three auditions a day. Today they're few and far between." To his credit, he does not insist that shrinking opportunities for playwrights are a violation of his constitutional rights. "The financial figures no longer made doing a play *on* Broadway a viable option," he reports dispassionately of his decision to produce *London Suite* Off-Broadway.

Simon's matter-of-fact acceptance of market-induced change is in keeping with his general demeanor, which is basically modest. He may emulate the great playwrights and drop names of Hollywood friends, but ultimately he comes across as a humble person who's surprised by what he has accomplished. Just inches away from modesty, though, is self-pity, and it is there that Simon sometimes descends as well. "[T]here comes a time when an actor doesn't have to audition," he observes. "If he's Tom Hanks or Jack Nicholson or Barbra Streisand, ad infinitum. I *always* have to audition. No star will do my play until he reads it first." And Simon unwisely considers his own status among playwrights, complaining that critics disapprove of him and designate him "Not Important" merely because he's popular.

An assessment of this kind should be left to others, though I'm not eager to assume the task myself. Making pronouncements about Neil Simon's place in the literary world is a thankless job. If entertaining an audience and rousing their emotions through honest storytelling are enough to make a writer important, then the author of *Lost in Yonkers* is an important playwright. But has Simon's work been critical to the development of modern drama? Has he helped set the course of the American theater? Does his material get under the skin of audience members? Do his entertainments amuse and delight so perfectly as to astonish?

Paradoxically, the uncontested renaming of an established Broadway house, the former Alvin Theater, in honor of Neil Simon, a living playwright, could be instructive: it suggests the author is not a threat to anyone. Simon may very well be the O. Henry of American drama. *Lost in Yonkers*, like "The Gift of the Magi," is at once widely admired and almost universally dismissed as not quite serious literature – precisely as Simon contends.

Unfortunately, the playwright has done nothing in this memoir to alter the consensus on his dramatic work. To put it bluntly, Simon is a barely passable prose stylist, and his editors have done him a disservice by overlooking numerous inaccurate citations and clichéd pronouncements. ("When time is limited, it is so much more precious.") A special irritant to me: Simon is positively obsessed with tabulating entertainment industry awards. By spending a significant period of his writing career on automatic pilot, and admitting it in his memoirs, Simon has not made the task of pursuing credibility any easier. If an author wishes his plays to be taken seriously, he should not liken his scripts to crusty breakfast food or himself to a well-made kitchen appliance.

[2002]

Moonlighting in Hollywood

In a 1997 interview, Nicky Silver confessed his impatience with playwrights who dabble in screenwriting but bristle at feedback from studio executives. "I don't buy writers who go, 'It's so horrible, they're so mean,'" Silver unloaded. "Then don't do it. Who's making you do it? You'll never, for instance, see a play from me about the vipers of Hollywood. They pay too well. It's hush money and you should just hush."

But like literature-professor novelists who publish book after book, story after story about the unique moral dilemmas faced by literature-professor novelists, our playwrights – even the most acclaimed – persistently examine their own shameful involvement in the film industry. The latest to turn his dramatic eye toward Hollywood is Craig Lucas, author of, among other plays, *Reckless* and *Prelude to a Kiss* as well as the film *Longtime Companion*. Lucas's most recent full-length play, *The Dying Gaul*, features Robert, a "wonderful writer" with "a beautiful visual sense," "a realistic understanding of forward action," and "an appreciation of the innate laws of storytelling as it directly relates to movie-making" – a bouquet of talents, we're told, shared by as few as twenty people in the entire world.

I found Lucas's writing in the opening scene surprisingly sharp, and quite daring considering that the audience is bound to associate mega-talented Robert with the author himself – or, rather, with the author's view of himself. It is daring for another reason: Lucas sets up a Faustian tale in which Robert is offered an obscene chunk of money for his screenplay – an even million dollars – so long as he compromises his work. Yet Lucas gives his Mephistopheles character every benefit of the doubt. Jeffrey, a bisexual studio executive, is no Hollywood moron: he has a clear eye for true talent and an accurate understanding of what will sell. "No one. Is going. To see. *The Dying Gaul*," he enunciates, referring to Robert's movie script, an autobiographical weepie about a writer whose male lover dies of AIDS. "I am sorry. Now. If we make Maurice a woman dying of AIDS ..."

Like an action film in which the president's airplane is hijacked, Lucas's play – or, rather, its premise – sounds overly familiar the first time we hear it. Still, the opening scene is so perfectly executed that we accept the derivative plot line without question. Robert, having just been told the studio is interested in producing his screenplay, cannot process the information at first. "Where else do you want to go with the script?" Jeffrey asks him.

> ROBERT: Well, I ... I guess I could take it to some of the independents.
> JEFFREY: No, no, no ... what a doll you are. What kind of work do you want to do on it?
> ROBERT: Oh. Oh, sorry ...
> JEFFREY: That's okay. That was just so sweet. From acceptance to total rejection, you took it all in stride.

Lucas is one of the few American playwrights with a natural ear for the rhythm and color of stage dialogue. "We will not make *The Dying Gaul* with two men in bed, falling in love, surviving pain and all the blah blah blah, it's not going to happen. Ever. Ever. Ever," Jeffrey explains. He counsels Robert, "Take the million and write something else." And despite a solemn promise to his recently deceased lover Malcolm not to heterosexualize the story, Robert succumbs.

For the first twelve pages of this 69-page script, then, Lucas is in top form. Unfortunately, the dilemma about compromising one's principles in Hollywood slips out of focus. Though Robert continues to work on script revisions with Jeffrey – and have sex with him – the emphasis of the play shifts from Robert's Faustian deal to his gradual acceptance of false signs of the supernatural. Robert confesses that he deals with his grief by wasting an inordinate amount of time in online chat rooms. Jeffrey's wife Elaine exploits this information to assume Malcolm's posthumous identity. Cyberchatting monopolizes the remainder of the play, with Robert and Elaine clicking away at their keyboards, narrating their instant messages for us.

"Where am I going with this?" Elaine asks about her deceit. It's a rhetorical question: her motivation is never usefully examined or clarified. Is she seeking revenge against her husband's lover? Or alleviating his grief? It's a bit muddled. Worse, Lucas feels the need to cover his back side by having Elaine utter asides to disguise the implausibilities of the plot and explain her prurient interest in this elaborate practical joke. ("It turns me on to hear people tell their experiences.")

From a combination of Buddhist enlightenment and psychotherapy, Robert believes he has been given the directive to kill this resurrected Malcolm, which he does. The play's violent ending was poorly received by both theater critics and a minority of colleagues whom Lucas consulted prior to mounting the play in New York City. The trade paperback in which *The Dying Gaul* appears, *What I Meant Was* (TCG, 1999), contains a preface and two afterwords by the author justifying his dramatic choices and insisting that any objections speak volumes about boorish gay commentators, cultural critics, and the "forces of reaction" – that is, about those leveling criticism at the playwright, not about the playwright himself. But I'm not so sure.

In several one-acts collected with *The Dying Gaul*, Lucas flirts with creating an environment of *Our Town*-like depth and poignancy for his deceased characters, but in the end he acquiesces to his true feelings: the grieving process, he suggests, is an appropriate occasion for survivors to send each other turds in boxes, literally or metaphorically. Throughout the past decade, Lucas has shirked the artist's responsibility to distance himself from the venomous impotence of his embittered characters. He has instead created nihilistic puppets whom he applauds for the authenticity of their (his) rage. "My lover, my best friend, my closest colleague over decades, my mother, my father-in-law and another several dozen friends, ex-lovers and colleagues all died rather horrible deaths in rapid succession," the author explains in the afterword to *The Dying Gaul*, "and I did not find myself ascending into a compassionate, giving place, but instead a significantly meaner and less generous one. And this play is the best I could make of my newfound insights." Fair enough. But it is disingenuous of the author to react so defensively when his plays – devoid of compassion and forgiveness – are critical failures. Like a brazen sexual outlaw who pounds on the door of the medical establishment demanding penicillin, Lucas flaunts conventional literary values but still expects to reap their professional benefits. I think he needs to make a decision and stick to it. My suggestion: no more turds in boxes.

Throughout *27 Short Plays* and *Collected Full-Length Plays: 1975–95*, Christopher Durang, like Craig Lucas, editorializes over his own work. But unlike Lucas, Durang is an engaging essayist. His staging instructions for "Mrs. Sorken" and "Sister Mary Ignatious Explains It All to You" are indispensable, his Yale Drama School gossip is compelling, and even his diatribes about being mishandled by drama critics at *The New York Times* build rather than weaken our esteem for his work. Unfortunately, Durang's most recent full-length play, *Betty's Summer Vacation* (Grove, 1999), is prefaced with comments by two colleagues. The foreword by Tim Sanford, artistic director of Playwrights Horizon where the play premiered, is particularly ill-conceived. "Hand me a play and tell me it's a hilarious satire on our tabloid culture and watch my eyes glaze over," he warns. "The targets are too easy."

Indeed they are, as Durang's play proves. *Betty's Summer Vacation* opens with the arrival at a beach house of the title character and Trudy, two woman in their late twenties who have taken a summer time-share. We learn immediately that Trudy is an insufferable chatterbox. But that gag gets dropped – *hard* – once the play declares its true purpose: exposing the corrosive influence of television news on our collective intelligence and the American legal system. "[F]or the first two pages or so, the play was kind of light," Durang states of his drafting experience in a self-interview, "but then on the third page a serial killer walked in – and, well, then the play changed." I found the change both abrupt and unwelcome. "I had had a period of watching Court TV a lot," Durang continues, "seeing much of the Menendez brothers' trial and the trial of Lorena Bobbit, who cut off her husband's penis while he slept – he sued her for bodily harm; and she sued him for being abusive to her in the past – and juries found them both innocent! Both. So nothing bad was done, apparently."

It's a clever point if you don't give it any thought. But, for starters, it was the plaintiff in each suit who faced the considerable burden of reasonable proof, which neither was able to surmount. Thus, it is understandable if separate juries arrived at what appear to be conflicting verdicts. "It was a real exercise in switching your point of view," a character in the play states about the Bobbit cases. That observation may apply to Christopher Durang, but not to the average television viewer who understands that our legal system is an attempt at delivering justice, not a guarantee of justice.

As always, Durang assembles a jumpy cast of characters including the lout-hunk Buck and the antisocial serial murderer Keith. A vagrant is welcomed into the household by the landlady Mrs. Siezmagraff who, it turns out, is Trudy's mother.

("But we don't talk much because her father incested her when he was drunk, and I never did anything about it because I was co-dependent.") And a chorus of three attached voices provides a laugh track and offstage commentary before crashing into the living room, demanding salacious entertainment or, at least, a bedtime story. Betty complies. "[A]t ten-forty-five," she ad libs, "the door bell of the castle rang, and in walked ... seven dwarfs, and a gnome, and a person with a hairlip."

> VOICE 2: This is starting to wake me up.
> VOICE 1: (*getting excited by his fantasy*) And the princess was really Andrew Cunanan in drag. And he killed all seven dwarfs, who were gay.
> VOICE 2: And the gnome collects shoes belonging to Marla Maples.
> VOICE 3: And the person with the hairlip is an S & M dominatrix who bites Marv Albert on the buttocks.
> VOICE 1: And then Frank Gifford has sex with Tonya Harding while Kathie Lee watches.
> VOICE 2: (*terribly happy*) And Amy Fisher has sex with Joey Buttafuoco and Charles Manson and a pig! And they make three TV movies about it!

Many of the play's madcap passages are funny once the chorus stops speaking in wit-deadening unison. But *Betty's Summer Vacation* – like Woody Allen's film *Celebrity* – offers no real insight into a tired subject. And, uncharacteristically, Durang includes a long, dull section in which the housemates play a game of charades that moves the plot nowhere.

Robert Brustein once described Durang, his former student, as "an angelic altar boy with poison leeching through his writing fingers." Like the novelist Bret Easton Ellis, Durang routinely exploits vulgar material for its sensational appeal yet remains distant and, like Ellis, a scold. I've long admired Durang's work and the expert way it parodies the absurd dialogue and blunt plot development of our most revered playwright, Eugene O'Neill. ("The baby's dead," announces an obstetrician in *The Marriage of Bette and Boo* before dropping the lifeless infant onto the hospital floor.) But Durang – like all satirists – runs the risk of piously elevating himself above the riffraff, which consists of other playwrights, the mentally ill, immediate family members, or anonymous television addicts, depending on the author's mood. If a satirist's observations, meant to be cutting and incisive, are merely obvious, he can look pretty silly. Compounding that problem, Durang has acted on stage in a number of his own productions, including *The Marriage of Bette and Boo* and *Laughing Wild* – two autobiographical works in which the Durang character provides a reservoir of conventional sanity in a world otherwise filled with babbling lunatics and emotional cripples.

Avoiding the "Great Deaf Ear" that was *New York Times* drama critic Frank Rich, Durang spent a good part of the late 1980s and early '90s writing screenplays and teleplays, many of them unproduced. His one-act "Business Lunch at the Russian Tea Room" features a playwright named Chris who meets a film development contact to discuss a screenwriting job. Everyone in the piece but Chris speaks in a scattered, absurd, or rude manner which casts a contrasting halo of decency and intelligence over the head of the playwright. It is probably ill-advised for any dramatist to write a Hollywood revenge satire or an exposé of tabloid sleaze, but either project is particularly perilous for Christopher Durang.

Neil Labute has made a name for himself not only as screenwriter but also as film director, most notably of *In the Company of Men*, a perfect first feature that offered a mercilessly caustic view of corporate America. "We may play it like a game sometimes, but believe me, a day doesn't go by in business that you're not out for somebody's blood," states the Young Man in "Iphigenia in Orem," the first of three one-acts constituting Labute's *Bash: Latterday Plays* (Overlook, 1999). From his Las Vegas hotel room, the Young Man admits he once exploited a vile opportunity to garner sympathy when a corporate takeover necessitated cuts in middle management. "I just kind of coaxed her down a bit," he confesses. "Down a bit further with the edge of my foot, turned her a touch and down and then I dropped the covers back and walked out." Having facilitated the suffocation death of his infant daughter, the Young Man maintains the gods are ultimately to blame: fate presented the opportunity, after all, and fate delayed his wife's return in time to save the child. In fact, the gods did have a cruel hand in tricking the Young Man with misinformation: it was not his head on the chopping block after all but, rather, that of a pushy female colleague. The daughter died for naught.

Does our culture actually place commerce above all else? Do we really value career advancement over family, over life itself? Or do we merely think we do because that's what we've been told by artists, churchmen, and foreign observers? I can imagine a European dramatist rewriting the story of Agamemnon sacrificing his own daughter, but I can't imagine a European updating it in quite the same way Labute has unless he set the play in America. Our blind avarice, it seems, has taken on the aura of universal truth.

Labute, a Mormon convert, assigned these "Latterday Plays" an all-Mormon cast of characters, sometimes to no effect, but sometimes to poor effect. In "A Gaggle of Saints," a bland college-aged couple – John and Sue – recount a recent trip to New York City where they attended a formal ball (the "bash" of the title) and where John and his male friends viciously attacked a stranger in Central Park (the "bash" of the title). I'm sure Mormons are as capable of evil as anyone, but here the young characters' sobriety and sense of responsibility to family and their own futures make an act of rash criminality perplexing and implausible.

What provokes the violence? This marauding pack of tuxedoed young men notices "two guys, middle-aged guys, L.L. Bean shirts on and the whole thing ... come out of the dark. Smiling." The only section of *Bash* not to mention a Greek character in its title, "A Gaggle of Saints" alludes to Oedipus. "One dude looks like my father, a little," John notes of the man he follows into a public restroom to pummel. "My first shot catches him against the cheek, just under the eye, " John reports dispassionately, as if still describing the group's mode of transportation or his date's new dress, "and he slams into a sink. All snot and blood running down. With so many of us hitting, tearing at him, it's hard to get off a clean punch but I know I connect a few more times. I feel his head, the back of it, softening as we go, but I just find a new spot and move on."

Frequent perusal of *The Washington Blade* or other serious gay publications suggests that persons committing acts of extreme violence against adult homosexuals generally fall into one of four categories: hustler-thieves (many of them gay), enraged boyfriends and ex-boyfriends (all of them gay), toothless hillbillies, and drunken frat boys. Since John and his buddies – proper Mormons all – do not fall within these groups, this orgy of violence is anachronistic. Labute is making an important point: gay bashing in American culture, he suggests, signals not a violation of societal norms but, rather, an adherence to societal norms. But I don't buy it, at least not in so literal and direct a manifestation as this. Religious groups cause emotional violence by forbidding "fornication" and "sodomy," but wilding of this sort is almost always the work of individuals who have slipped outside the influence of their culture and its moral instruction.

Labute's concluding one-act, "Medea Redux," gives everything away in the title. The play's only character, an unnamed woman in her late twenties, relates prior misadventures with her junior high science instructor, who encouraged her to carry his baby to term, then abandoned her. Fourteen years later, she tracks him down and introduces him to his teenage son. "He was satisfied," she recounts, appalled by the man's good fortune. "I could see that, satisfaction on his face ... because he'd gotten away with it all. That's what I saw, shining in his eyes, as he moved forward to kiss me. He'd beaten fate ... and gotten away with it."

I excuse all implausibilities here, as I do in Euripides' *Medea*, and make the same rationalizations on behalf of the playwright: the main character is not right in the head, I tell myself; she's determined to cut off her nose to spite her face; there's logic in her behavior, after all, for she derives greater satisfaction from watching the man suffer than from killing him outright.

As in the other two sections of *Bash*, Labute indulges in a bit of throat clearing before he gets to the confession. But I have no major qualms with this third piece, other than the fact that so much monologuing, with no dramatization, grows predictably wearisome. "Iphigenia in Orem" and "Medea Redux" feature one performer each. "A Gaggle of Saints" has two characters, John and Sue, but each addresses us directly. Labute seems confident his solo writing delivers as much narrative tension and catharsis as a dramatic play. But as the Greek dramatists realized over time, it rarely does.

I cannot confirm if Richard Greenberg, the prolific author most recently of *Hurrah at Last*, regularly moonlights in Hollywood. But I doubt it. Greenberg has been labeled a "working playwright"; *Hurrah at Last* (included in *Three Days of Rain and Other Plays*, Grove Press, 1999) is his fourth commission from South Coast Repertory. The play's focus is Laurie, a talented but indigent novelist who lives "from tiny windfall to tiny windfall," leeching off more affluent relatives who see him through as long as he doesn't say anything too truthful.

Laurie's profitably married sister, Thea, and her husband Eamon throw a Christmas party for the siblings' parents, Laurie's devoted friend Oliver, and Oliver's fertile wife Gia. But amid the preparations, Laurie can't get his mind off the subject of money. It unnerves him that dutiful Oliver – a popular hack playwright – would drop his pants if Laurie asked, but he will not tell Laurie how wealthy he is. "How much money do *you* have?" Laurie asks Thea, since he's on the subject.

> THEA: I'm not going to tell you *that*.
> LAURIE: You're my sister, we shared a womb –
> THEA: We're not twins –
> LAURIE: It was a *time*-share; how much money do you have?

The womb, like money, is a recurring motif in the play: Gia gets pregnant every time Oliver looks at her, while Thea and Eamon have repeatedly failed with *in vitro* fertilization.

> THEA: Laurie, we tried again last week.
> LAURIE: What? Oh.
> THEA: It didn't take.
> LAURIE: Oh. I'm sorry.
> THEA: There's no baby. We have to start all over again.
> LAURIE: Oh God, that's so expensive, I mean heartbreaking.

Soon after the guests arrive, Laurie collapses from a hard-to-diagnose medical condition and spends the majority of the play in a state of delirium. Born into a world where talentless beauties like Oliver enjoy a financial windfall from mere dreck, Laurie feels his paranoia mount while prone on a hospital bed, particularly after his mother carelessly tells him he's moribund.

> LAURIE: People are telling me *every*thing, right? I mean ... I'm not ... moribund ... am I?
> THEA: Certainly *not*. (*She pats his head*.) ... Of course, we don't really *know* anything, yet.
> LAURIE: Thea – !
> THEA: And they *do* keep sending in that rabbi.
> LAURIE: Thea?
> THEA: *Death*, though ...
>   (*She lets it hang*.)
> LAURIE: *What?*
> THEA: When you think about it, death ... is really relative, isn't it?
> LAURIE: No.

Greenberg's 1997 drama *Three Days of Rain* remains his finest play, but *Hurrah at Last* shares many of its qualities, including a solid structure, bright dialogue, and a cast of privileged New Yorkers. Here, in a screwball comedy, the playwright wisely makes financial concerns a desperate obsession of the main character. ("I SAID: I DON'T HAVE ANY MONEY!") What could be sillier than a talented, upper-middle-class white guy worrying about destitution? Well – perhaps a Jewess who loves Christmas, but whose favorite holiday is Easter. Or a happily married heterosexual playwright platonically in love with his gay best friend.

Should we attempt to locate the kernel of substance buried deep within the frivolity of Greenberg's play? All of Western literature, it must be said, is at some basic level a frivolous entertainment, no matter how edifying, educational, somber, or ambitious. It doesn't feed anyone, it cures no disease. Greenberg accepts this without fuss. His characters are witty, attractive, selectively affectionate – and largely admirable if we disregard their failure to heed Christ's imperative to sell their possessions and donate the proceeds to the poor. (Laurie, in fact, goes into a panic when told his Catholic brother-in-law has done just that.) Greenberg wisely chooses not to preach to the theater audience, themselves a privileged lot. Righteous indignation is the cheapest emotion one can inflame in a crowd, but I'm not convinced it stimulates action or even careful thought. Rather, it seems most often to work as a safety valve for venting liberal guilt. Richard Greenberg does nothing to diminish the material inequities of our culture by exploiting them for laughs, but neither, I suppose, does he make the situation any worse.

And, in the meantime, we get to enjoy his considerable gifts. Like Bruce Bawer in his poetry, Peter Cameron in his short fiction, and Andrew Sullivan in his personal essays, Richard Greenberg in his dramatic works never overestimates how interesting others will find his writing. This may not be a quality common to our greatest literary artists – in fact, it may not apply to any great literary artist – but it is a most welcome quality in a playwright one wishes to recommend to a friend.

Curiously, *Hurrah at Last* grows in stature upon re-reading. *Three Days of Rain* has an ingenious plot twist at the end that, like the famous last line of *Long Day's Journey into Night*, we subsequently remember as having seemed ingenious the first time we heard it, but the effect of which weakens with time and repeated exposure. *Hurrah at Last*, for all its manic silliness, only grows more delightful. It is an amusing confection and further proof of an already obvious talent.

[2002]

Tennessee Williams on the Incline

"Who can presume to know what is best for genius?" asked John Uecker in Lyle Leverich's *Tom: The Unknown Tennessee Williams* as he cast a backward glance at the playwright's tortured final days in 1983. Ailing and depressed, Williams refused to eat, take medication, or seek hospitalization; his friends – Uecker among them – felt helpless to interfere. "A man like that you do not treat like a regular person," Uecker explained.

If the documents collected in the first volume of *The Selected Letters of Tennessee Williams* (New Directions, 2000) are a reliable indication, Tom Williams was masquerading as a merely talented and ambitious young writer – that is, a regular person – until others branded him a genius at the age of thirty-four following the Broadway premier of his first masterpiece ("I think it contains my sister"). A second volume of letters will follow, but the early period covered here turns out to be, as is nearly always the case, the most exciting in the writer's life. (*A Moveable Feast* and *Breakfast at Tiffany's*, in their variously fictionalized forms, attest to this truth.) These are the innocent years before success throws an author into competition with himself: literature is endlessly fascinating, love seems possible, body and mind are sound, and the arc of one's career is ascendant. An aura of newness touches everything; innumerable virginities are lost.

Like Tom Wingfield in *The Glass Menagerie*, the young Williams fled his family for the refuge of artistic creation, fame, and material success. Much of this same ground is covered by the playwright in his *Memoirs* (1975), but inaccurately and ineptly. In contrast to Arthur Miller's magisterial and important autobiography, *Timebends* (1987), *Memoirs* is an embarrassment to its author and serves as further proof, if more were needed, that Williams went into irreversible decline as a writer following *The Night of the Iguana* in 1961. Anecdotes first recorded in these letters lose their vitality when repeated in the drug-damaged *Memoirs*.

In the letters it is amusing to read that a Mrs. Wingfield used to stack the storeroom of the author's maternal grandparents' home in Clarksdale, MS; that a co-worker at the Continental Shoemakers warehouse in St. Louis was named Stanley Kowalski; and that the young Williams wrote a one-sentence letter to Harriet Monroe, editor of *Poetry* magazine, asking: "Will you do a total stranger the kindness of reading his verse?" But these letters afford more profound insight than that into both the author's personal life and the turbulent process of writing his first three professionally produced plays: the doomed *Battle of Angels* (later reworked as *Orpheus Descending* and the film *The Fugitive Kind*), *The Glass Menagerie*, and – at the very end of the book – *A Streetcar Named Desire*.

Born Thomas Lanier Williams III in 1911 – a year after his sister Rose was born – the aspiring author was by his mid-twenties a prolific dramatist, poet, and short story writer as well as a dutiful correspondent. In fact, his obsessive yet scattershot writing habits may have delayed his professional success. He informs his mother from the road in May 1939: "The Group Theatre and my new agent, Audrey Wood, both urge me to devote all my time to writing one long, careful play as they feel I have been working too rapidly and without sufficient concentration on one thing." Later that year, hard at work on *Battle of Angels*, he informs Molly Day Thacher, playreader at the Group Theatre and the future wife of director Elia Kazan: "My method of writing is terrifically wasteful. I have already written enough dialogue for two full-length plays, some of the best of which will have to be eliminated because it flies off on some inessential tangent." About the tiresome revision process he concludes: "For an intelligent writer this would not be much of a problem but I must admit I am not. My attack is purely emotional."

Of course at the peak of his powers Williams was a fiercely intelligent writer; but it is instructive to read the author's early dismissal of his own ability to shape a play or tame emotional excess with intellectual rigor. Now renowned for the poetry of his dialogue and the tangential arias of his major female characters, Williams seems to have made a virtue of his weakness.

Battle of Angels starring Miriam Hopkins premiered December 30, 1940, in Boston. Though produced by the prestigious Theatre Guild, the production was a disaster, and it closed in two weeks. Lyle Leverich suggests in his biography that Boston, with its infamous tradition of censorship, was an inauspicious choice for the out-of-town run of so highly erotic a play. But the playwright's own account explains the premiere's poor reception thus: "Unfortunately all of the first-string critics went to Gertrude Lawrence's show [*Lady in the Dark*] which opened the same night and we got a bunch of prissy old maids to write our notices."

Leverich also asserts that Williams was largely indifferent to the success of *Battle of Angels* and was therefore unwilling to make changes to an ill-conceived script. The epistolary evidence doesn't bear Leverich out. Two months after the play closed, Williams tells his agent that he is putting aside a new short story to try to salvage *Battle of Angels* for a possible New York production. Earlier, during the build up to Boston, the playwright assures Theresa Helburn of the Theatre Guild that her ideas for reshaping the script coincide with his own, even while he complains to his mother that the Guild's revision requirements – which he honors – are basically "foolish." And Williams blames the play's ultimate failure on his overwillingness to revise. "The play is not ready for New York," he admits during the Boston run, "due mostly to my ill-advised efforts to make it a starring vehicle satisfactory to Miss Hopkins rather than to my own best judgment."

We are getting only half of the story here, and an often unreliable and self-contradictory half – which, of course, is the fun of reading a one-sided correspondence. "My work is hard to sell," Williams warns his mother in 1941, "on account of not being written so much for commercial as artistic aims." Yet he repeatedly reassures his agent he is willing to recast his ideas in whatever form – short story, play, novel – is most likely to attract an editor or producer. In August 1942 he admits that his D.H. Lawrence adaptation, *You Touched Me!*, was "written to make me some money to live on." And his enthusiasm for profit seems to have peaked while drafting *Battle of Angels*. "I *do* think this play is *Commercial!*" he gushes to Audrey Wood. "Capital 'C' as in CASH!"

From the letters we can trace Williams's path around North America as he avoided his family in St. Louis but grew restless everywhere else that he tried to settle: New York City; Hollywood; Jacksonville, Florida; Macon, Georgia; Key West. From New Orleans he jokes to Paul Bigelow about having to move. "A misunderstanding about some sailors who come in occasionally to discuss literature with me provoked a tedious little quarrel with the land-lady – I told her I could not live in such an atmosphere of unwarranted suspicion." From New York he discusses with Joe Hazan the poet Clark Mills's suicidal tendencies. "I reasoned with him for a long time about the infinite value of life, of the miracle of simply being alive, and through this I think I convinced myself of it." And in Acapulco, Mexico – while writing *Battle of Angels* – he drafts a long anti-Nazi screed triggered by the presence of German tourists who were celebrating the bombing of London. This impassioned piece, quoted at length in Leverich's biography, helps correct the misconception that Williams was politically detached and uninformed. In fact, most of Williams's early full-length dramas – *Stairs to the Roof*, *Candles to the Sun*, *Not About Nightingales* – conform to the 1930s definition of politically engaged theater.

Nevertheless that did not satisfy everyone. In 1942, the Studio Theatre, under the helm of émigré director Erwin Piscator, announced plans to mount a revised *Battle of Angles*, but negotiations on the script broke down. The bitter sarcasm in Williams's account of a meeting with the hypocritical Piscator is illuminating. "I arrived at this palatial estate on the Hudson, admitted by a Prussian butler," he fumes to Audrey Wood. "[Piscator] was lying up in bed with his dinner tray. Over the bed was a fur robe – I believe it was mink – and he was wearing peach-colored silk pyjamas. He looked at me mournfully and said, 'Mr. Williams, you have written a Fascist play – all of your characters are selfishly pursuing their little personal ends and aims in life with a ruthless disregard for the wrongs and sufferings of the world about them.'" With understandable eagerness to reach the New York stage, Williams could easily have buckled under the director's demands for more "epic" theater, but the playwright stood firm. "Mr. Piscator is a terribly dictatorial German," he concludes to his mother, "completely impractical, and is trying to force me to turn the play into a dry, didactic sermon on social injustice, representing the South as a fascist state."

The letters make clear that in 1942 Williams put himself on a successful professional course, risking charges of decadence and worse by protecting his artistic vision. Yet success would come only with great effort: his next play – entitled "The Gentleman Caller" through much of its drafting – meandered through numerous ill-advised configurations, including a film treatment. In August 1943 the author describes his dubious progress to Audrey Wood: he has given the tragic drama a happy ending. Finally the playwright, having guided the project safely into port, sends director Margo Jones news of the play's completion. "It has some interesting new techniques," he informs her, "and all in all I am not displeased with the out-come. That is, when I consider the terrible, compulsive struggle it was to do the thing and what a frightful, sentimental mess it might well have been, and was at some stages."

What's missing from the author's correspondence is a blow-by-blow account of the rehearsals in December 1944 for the Chicago run of *The Glass Menagerie* and its successful transfer three months later to Broadway. From Leverich's biography we know there was plenty of amusing material to relate – the absurdity of forty-nine-year-old Eddie Dowling playing a young man itching to declare independence from his mother; or star Laurette Taylor's inexpert southern accent, likened by several observers to Tennessee's own affected manner of speech. But the author was too preoccupied to correspond. "What a hectic time!" he squeezes into a six-line note to his grandfather on Christmas Day. We get only a brief summary in a March letter to his publisher, Jay Laughlin: "Pandemonium backstage! Intrigues, counter-intrigues, rages, smashed door-panes, – quelle menagerie!"

Also missing are extended comments about the author's taste in drama, his influences and rivalries. Leverich informs us that Williams found Eugene O'Neill's writing in *Desire Under the Elms* "incredibly bad," but few such observations surface here. Williams sends fan letters to William Saroyan, Katherine Anne Porter, and Clifford Odets, and asks after a new discovery, Fred Rothermell, author of the thirties proletarian story "Vain Voyage." But I wanted more. "I regard [Horton] Foote with a somewhat uncharacteristic reserve," he finally admits to Audrey Wood. "Rivalry has something to do with it, I'm sure." His direct verbal attacks are aimed at random recipients, such as Joan Crawford, who was originally offered the Hopkins role in *Battle of Angels* ("She is such a '*ham*'!"), and the public librarian in Macon, Georgia: "Miss Sally Aikins is a *horrid* little person – *venomous*? My *God!*" As that quotation suggests, the author slips into the Raging Queen mode on occasion, though mostly with close friends Paul Bigelow and Joe Hazan, who also receive updates on the author's sexual exploits. "The evils of promiscuity are exageratted [sic]," he tells – of all people – his publisher. "Somebody said it has at least the advantage of making you take more baths."

And there is one deafening silence: Williams rarely inquires about his sister Rose once he reaches adulthood. Institutionalized in 1937 with schizophrenia, Rose was subjected to a bilateral prefrontal lobotomy in 1943, which her mother informed Tom of after the fact. Williams seems to have saved his remorse for his journal and, of course, *The Glass Menagerie*, which drew widespread attention to the playwright's relationship to his family.

"[T]he public Somebody you are when you 'have a name' is a fiction created with mirrors," Williams laments in his famous essay "The Catastrophe of Success" (1947). But subterfuge helped to shape the young unknown Williams as well. For this reason, the editors of *Selected Letters* – Albert J. Devlin and Nancy M. Tischler – have augmented Williams's correspondence with what they call "a running commentary to separate Williams's sometimes hilarious, but often devious, counter-reality from truth."

And it is a remarkable job they've done. Having first winnowed down some 900 extant letters, notes, and telegrams to the 330 published here in their entirety, Devlin and Tischler provide annotations drawn from letters passed over for full inclusion, correspondence from the Williams family and the playwright's agent, Lyle Leverich's research, an FBI file on Williams released under the Freedom of Information Act, and the author's journals (which are forthcoming from Yale University Press). These help cover the gaps mentioned above. The editors' efforts, in fact, approach Leverich's own for thoroughness; their book, in turn, offers a biographical record rivaling his in comprehensiveness, but with greater immediacy and sharper focus. A healthy plurality of the playwright's letters are addressed to four key persons: his mother, his agent, his publisher, and Paul Bigelow. The only major omission is a prudent one: because *Tennessee Williams' Letters to Donald Windham 1940–1965* was published in 1976, only one (unsent) letter to Windham, the playwright's friend and collaborator on *You Touched Me!*, is included here.

Three years after *The Glass Menagerie* catapulted Williams to fame and fortune, he romanticized the time chronicled in *Selected Letters* as years spent "clawing and scratching along a sheer surface and holding on tight with raw fingers." In reality his existence was not nearly so precarious, at least financially. For one thing he had no trouble securing a first-rate agent who, in 1943, landed him a contract with Metro-Goldwyn-Mayer, where his assignments included adapting a trashy novel for Lana Turner's next film project. ("I feel like an obstetrician required to successfully deliver a mastodon from a beaver.") Exaggerated claims made by the playwright in subsequent years can now be checked against these contemporary accounts which, while not strictly truthful, at least give us a picture of a fully human author untainted by the aura of genius. It is simply fascinating to watch an embryonic playwright who cannot predict which works will remain in the bottom drawer (*Not About Nightingales*), which will flop (*Battle of Angles*), and which will hijack his life and alter the course of modern drama.

Ending as it does in 1945, just as Williams commences drafting *A Streetcar Named Desire* amid the din of success from *The Glass Menagerie*, this volume boasts the standard three-part structure of a solid narrative work – initial struggle, second-act failure, final-curtain triumph – but it also has a forward-looking ending that finds the successful young author still shaping his most famous play. "At the moment it has four different titles, The Moth, The Poker Night, The Primary Colors, or Blanche's Chair In The Moon," Williams writes to Audrey Wood. "It is about two sisters, the remains of a fallen southern family. The younger, Stella, has accepted the situation, married beneath her socially and moved to a southern city with her coarsely attractive, plebian mate." As of March 1945, Williams is still considering three possible endings.

> One, Blanche simply leaves – with no destination.
> Two, goes mad.
> Three, throws herself in front of a train in the freight-yards.

One feels irrational concern, reading these letters, for Blanche DuBois and Stanley Kowalski, whose fates must yet be fixed – whose very names must still be settled on – before they can enter the pantheon of dramatic immortals. "The place is finally lost, Belle-reve," Williams continues, "and Blanche, destitute, gives up the struggle and takes refuge with Stella in the southern city. She arrives broken by the failing struggle (arrival first scene of play) and is at the mercy of the tough young husband, Ralph."

[2002]

DAVID MAMET IN THEORY AND PRACTICE

David Mamet's publication record challenges the widely accepted falsehood that the value of a playwright's professional stock plummets if he is perceived as prolific. Over the past three decades, Mamet has written more than twenty original full-length plays. In addition, he has published numerous adaptations, two volumes of prose fiction, two poetry collections, several children's books, eight volumes of nonfiction, and fourteen screenplays. In 1999 alone, he premiered a new play and published a collection of poetry, two screenplays, and his fifth collection of short essays, *Jafsie and John Henry* (Free Press, 1999). He also directs feature films.

Mamet's short essays focus on a fixed constellation of topics: drama, masculine pursuits (card playing, hunting, drinking, friendship), the American Jewish identity, and childhood memories. He has further developed his observations on theater and movies in *On Directing Film* (1991), the provocative acting manual *True and False* (1997), and *Three Uses of the Knife* (1998), an examination of "the nature and purpose of drama."

In a 1984 interview, Mamet asserted that the well-made play imitated the structure of human cognition. The author expands on this point in *Three Uses of the Knife*. "Dramatic structure," he writes, "is not an arbitrary – or even a conscious – invention. It is an organic codification of the human mechanism for ordering information. Event, elaboration, denouement; thesis, antithesis, synthesis; boy meets girl, boy loses girl, boy gets girl; act one, two, three." This anti-Foucauldian view of cultural norms (he claims they have biological rather than sinister or arbitrary origins) is rooted in a naked desire to please the audience. Drama, Mamet concluded long ago, is good for one thing only: telling a story. And people are naturally receptive to a story with a beginning, middle, and end. The only people who do not conceive of stories in this manner, he notes, are experimental, anti-mimetic playwrights.

Mamet's considerable experience in theater, filtered through the theses of Bruno Bettelheim's *The Uses of Enchantment*, has led him to conclude that the theater artist's task is to ease the disparity between the conscious and unconscious minds – "to cure a raging imbalance" – and so achieve peace. Dramatic form facilitates this task. It permits the playwright to address questions the conscious mind is incompetent to deal with. Ideally, when dramatic structure is employed expertly in a play, it brings the subconscious and conscious into alignment, at which point the audience feels it has to hear what happens next.

By contrast, a didactic play – a drama that poses a question we can answer rationally, like "Are black people deserving of respect?" – makes us feel diverted but not fulfilled. "It might make a good tract, it might make a good political platform, it might make a good speech. But it can't be art," Mamet writes. By appealing only to the rational mind, the "problem play" fails to grip audience members at a deeper level of consciousness. At most, it instills in them a sense of superiority to those characters whose actions they recognize as morally repugnant.

These are ideas Mamet has been developing for some time. In *On Directing Film*, he wrote: "People have tried for centuries to use drama to change people's lives, to influence, to comment, to express themselves. It doesn't work. It might be nice if it worked for those things, but it doesn't." In *True and False*, he offered this bit of heresy: "Our theater is clogged with plays about Important Issues; playwrights and directors harangue us with right-thinking views on many topics of the day. But these are, finally, harangues, they aren't drama, and they aren't fun to do. The audience and the actor nod in acquiescence, [...] but it is a corruption of the theatrical exchange." I welcome Mamet's doggedness on this issue, which *is* heresy, and which explains the paradoxical situation contemporary theater finds itself in. By addressing "relevant issues," theater risks making itself irrelevant to the human psyche.

"Always do things in the least interesting way," Mamet wrote in *On Directing Film*, "and you make a better movie." By that, he meant that attempts to tart up a character – assigning adverbs in the script or mugging on stage – merely distract attention from the story, which is of paramount interest. Mamet's appreciation for simplicity is evident in his plays, which read briskly, in part because he does not invite cheap histrionics from performers. Everything is on the page: in the story and in the language. Canvassing Mamet's dramatic oeuvre, however, I found passages where the author places perhaps too much faith in pure narrative, which a literate audience might fully anticipate, particularly in the strictly Aristotelian form Mamet favors, tragedy. It may be impossible for Mamet to bring the audience's conscious and unconscious minds into alignment if audience members have grown impatient with the characters.

"Endings in tragedies are resolved," Mamet explained to Matthew C. Roudané in 1984. "The protagonist undergoes a reversal of the situation, a recognition of the state, and we have a certain amount of cleansing. This is what Don experiences in *American Buffalo*. But this doesn't happen in *Glengarry Glen Ross*. So the structure is different. It's not as classical a play as *Buffalo*, and it's probably not as good a play." Anyone familiar with both works knows, in fact, that *Glengarry Glen Ross* is far superior to *American Buffalo*, a tragedy whose resolution demands a stubborn obtuseness from its characters. For instance, Don, the pawnshop owner who is planning a minor heist, has failed to notice that one of his poker buddies – the one who keeps winning – is a habitual cheater. Don also lacks even ballpark knowledge of the value of rare coins passing through his store and can't be bothered to investigate their worth. In Mamet's work, the more urgent the dramatic point, the more implausible the setup. In *Edmond*, the title character's abrupt descent into poverty, hopelessness, and murder rests on his gullibility and a convenient lapse into insanity.

When I say the audience grows impatient with the characters, I do not mean the audience can predict the precise details of the reversal the protagonist will undergo. But they know he will undergo a reversal of some sort – they've read Aristotle, too. And they know it will not be triggered by an arbitrary cataclysm beyond the protagonist's control, as in a melodrama, but rather by the protagonist's own actions, à la Oedipus. Too often, Mamet resorts to a simple slip of the tongue. In *The Cryptogram*, Del tells Donny her husband gave him a knife as a memento on a camping trip, which Donny knows is a lie. In *Glengarry Glen Ross*, Levene chews out his boss on behalf of a colleague, and in so doing implicates himself in an office burglary. Mamet strains the audience's credulity by placing too much weight on this Freudian crutch. (Levene: "I'm halfway hoping to get caught.") In the most extreme cases, we get an I-Just-Can't-Help-Myself-I-Have-To-Blurt-This-Out scene. Karen, the conniving temporary office assistant in *Speed-the-Plow*, is asked by an angry professional rival if she would have slept with her boss had he not approved her film proposal. "No," she admits, "No." The problem is not simply that Karen instantly converts to a life of self-defeating honesty – her admission loses her the film deal – but that the other characters fully expect her to. They seem sympathetic to the bind the author is in, and are willing to play along.

The problem Mamet faces is not merely one of formalist exhaustion. The weakness of implausibility was inherent from the very beginning of drama, even in Aristotle's model of the tragic form, Sophocles' *Oedipus Rex*. As a character in Richard Greenberg's *Three Days of Rain* comically notes, "[I]f some oracle told you you were going to kill your father and marry your mother, wouldn't you just never kill anyone and stay single? ... Wouldn't you be smart enough to, like, avoid older women?" Characters in tragedy are never smart enough, and in Mamet's plays they are downright imbecilic. (Don in *American Buffalo*: "What are you doing here?" Bob: "I came here.") This is, in part, because real human beings act self-destructively (that is, stupidly) and because drama takes its logic from dream narrative. The protagonist's actions are driven by a vertigo-like pull, inevitably drawing the character over the side of a cliff. This is not smart behavior, but it is dramatic.

Still, the implausibilities and irritations remain. Mamet acknowledges that third act problems are nearly inevitable in playwriting and he pleads for understanding: "It is much easier to write great dialogue [...] than to write great plots." Mamet's disjointed dialogue is the most renowned feature of his writing, and I believe it stems from problems inherent in his work. The following exchange between two real estate salesmen in *Glengarry Glen Ross* is not exactly typical of Mamet's dialogue, which is not as relentlessly elliptical and choppy as some think, but it is prototypical:

> AARONOW: We're stuck with *this* ...
> MOSS: We're stuck with *this* fucking shit ...
> AARONOW: ... *this* shit ...
> MOSS: It's too ...
> AARONOW: It is.
> MOSS: Eh?
> AARONOW: It's too ...
> MOSS: You get a bad month, all of a ...
> AARONOW: You're on this ...
> MOSS: All of, they got you on this "board" ...
> AARONOW: I, I ... I ...

MOSS: Some *contest* board ...
AARONOW: I ...
MOSS: It's not right.

Mamet describes his dialogue as "poetic," "musical," "tailor-made for the stage." It is indeed all those things. My concern is the extent to which educated or streetwise characters are forced to sound incoherent to lend plausibility to their ignorant, self-destructive actions. Mamet's characters stutter in the service of tragic form.

Mamet's staccato language surfaces in his nonfiction as well, in the blunt, single-sentence paragraphs his essays often comprise. Perhaps because he developed his recent theorizing on drama to book length in *Three Uses of the Knife*, Mamet's latest collection of short essays, *Jafsie and John Henry*, includes relatively few observations on theater. Mamet focuses instead on the tendency of Jewish Americans toward self-loathing, the male-female divide, and his nostalgia for youth from the vantage point of middle age.

In a previous collection, Mamet said of specifically masculine activities like boxing, gambling, and shooting: "I have sought them out and enjoy them all vastly. They are times that I cherish." He has also asserted that men and women do not want the same things, and that female colleagues, in his professional experience, have consistently demonstrated the cruelest and most arrogant behavior because they are less fearful of censure from peers. In his latest collection, Mamet balks at the sloppy use of the word *macho* to mean anything male and, therefore, "degenerate and ludicrous," and he condemns attempts by women to infantilize men by demanding they become "emotionally responsive." Statements of this ilk have won Mamet numerous detractors, as has the fierce language of his volatile male characters ("Southern bulldyke asshole ingrate of a vicious nowhere cunt"). But he has his defenders as well. British playwright Rebecca Prichard, considering the recent crop of arbitrarily violent male plays in London, notes that those works owe little to Mamet's dramatic writing, which does not celebrate nihilism or even masculinity, but which explores the link between society's values and its brutality.

If Mamet acquits himself on gender, he has less success with the issues of Judaism and the American Jewish identity, which seem only to make him crabby. It is instructive, considering Mamet's distaste for melodrama, to read his dismissal of *Schindler's List* as "an exploitation film" and "emotional pornography." But pronouncements like "We are a beautiful people and a good people" do not belong among the mature writings of a significant literary talent. They are the Jewish rejoinder to Kwanzaa propaganda, and are better left to educators, the talentless, and the well-intentioned.

Similarly, Mamet makes occasionally airless declarations about popular culture that echo the work of our laziest academics: Disneyland is best understood as a totalitarian state, for example. The author has written of his wasted undergraduate years at a college with an unstructured curriculum where, essentially, no learning took place. He still suffers from lost time. This is especially obvious in his essays on economic matters – works informed almost exclusively by the theories of Thorstein Veblen. For years, Mamet's dramatic writing triumphed by tapping into a theatrical zeitgeist that was similarly ill-informed. Mamet's most successful works can, I believe, be fairly encapsulated thus: sex workers, pawnshop owners, pimps, and "legitimate" salesmen of all kinds use coercive techniques to bilk the customer. And they are willing to abandon even the thin patina of legality and resort to violence if necessary. The heartless economic system forces them to do so. Mamet has long been fascinated and unnerved by "the American myth," which he defines as the expectation of getting something for nothing and which he views as the basis of our economic life. "And this also affects the spirit of the individual. It's very divisive. One feels one can only succeed at the cost of someone else."

Mamet's skepticism defers to "the European myth" espoused for decades by the Social Democratic Left, who insisted that the prosperity of an individual arose inevitably at the expense of the collective. Recent economic developments worldwide now confirm that affluence is generally beneficial – a point no longer lost even on the Social Democrats. The most important question looming over Mamet's career concerns this altered zeitgeist: Will the author conform subsequent dramatic works to a post-Thatcherite world of New Labour and "Third Way" economics?

I hope Mamet continues in his nonfiction to serve as a thoughtful amalgamator of theories first espoused by others – Aristotle, Eisenstein, Bettelheim, even Stanislavsky, whose acting method Mamet now dismisses. But the author is clearly in a transitional period in his dramatic work, both regarding his primary choice of media – he works more frequently in film now than theater – and in subject matter. Mamet's plays from the nineties, including *The Cryptogram* and *The Old Neighborhood*, suggest the author is drawing upon childhood for inspiration and plot material. That's fine, as long as it is a sign of aging and nostalgia, not of timidity or confusion. Mamet may voice questionable generalizations about society, but the fierceness of his convictions is what lent his earlier dramas their energy. His small sin was to misdirect his ire at a faceless political and economic establishment that could not reasonably be expected to rescue characters bent on classically tragic self-ruin. It is a graver sin – and an unsavory spectacle – for the playwright to redirect his venom toward his parents now that our general economic predicament appears less dire.

If Mamet needs material for a socially engaged drama in the post-Cold War economy, I suggest he consult some of the more vital passages in his own nonfiction for inspiration. "Our undeniable Puritan society can countenance chastity and pornography, but little in between," he writes in "Scotch Malt Whisky Society" from *Jafsie and John Henry*. "It seems we have a problem with the issue of control."

In *Three Uses of the Knife*, he states, "The avant-garde is to the left what jingoism is to the right. Both are a refuge in nonsense."

And in the preface to *Jafsie and John Henry*, he affirms the artist's wish not to embarrass himself. Paradoxically for a playwright, this means resisting the social contract and saying the unacceptable. Things get complicated, however, if the rebellious author wins attention and acclaim. "Success ratifies the iconoclast, and places him or her in the strange position of having been endorsed for being a detractor," Mamet notes.

I can think of no subject matter more vital to today's theater than this inverted social contract. A playwright ingratiates himself to the establishment these days by screaming curses at the powers that be. It is nearly impossible to voice something unacceptable anymore unless one remains doggedly square and sober. Mamet would seem to be the perfect playwright to grapple with this material, having had the bad taste in the past to dismiss performance art and "women's writing" as decadent and elitist, and having gone on record bemoaning the effects of government arts funding. The author is clearly at a professional crossroads. I cite as evidence his recent film, an adaptation of Terrence Rattigan's *The Winslow Boy*, which Mamet describes as "a work of melodramatic genius." That one of America's more prolific and original writers should resort to filming an adaptation in a genre he openly deplores suggests confusion.

Or perhaps it signals a change of heart. Perhaps David Mamet has loosened up and is willing to ease his adherence to a strictly Aristotelian approach to drama. Perhaps we can expect articulate, plainspoken characters from him in the future – intelligent people to whom bad things occasionally happen, rather than ignorant louts who keep mucking up their own lives. If so, David Mamet is my choice to lead American playwrights through the wilderness of political and bureaucratic confusion, face up to the surprisingly benign nature of our economic system, and point us toward a new century of American drama.

[2000]

The Goldilocks Formula

In an early essay, Susan Sontag expressed admiration – or was it dismay? – at playwright Peter Weiss's "staggering ambition" to combine dicta from twentieth-century drama's two major theorists, Bertolt Brecht and Antonin Artaud, in his masterpiece *Marat/Sade*. Both Weiss's ambition and Sontag's reaction now seem indicative of the mid-1960s, when an artist could attach himself to defiant aesthetic principles and still wear a pleased, unironic look on his face. In a new volume, *The Playwright's Guidebook* (Faber and Faber, 2002), Stuart Spencer leaps over the incautious essays of Brecht and Artaud – plus a good many others – and appropriates from Aristotle's *Poetics* the bases of an instruction manual for young dramatists. Spencer's work, too, is suggestive of its moment: we are entering a new century of drama, it tells us, in need of replenishment.

The decision to omit Artaud's avant-garde theories from a drama primer was a no-brainer: Artaud repudiated Western theater because of its dependence on literary texts, whereas Spencer's task is to facilitate the production of dramatic literature. "It's language, really," he concludes about drama, sending Artaud spinning in his grave. "It's words." The decision to omit Brecht's theories on alienation, which uproot Aristotle's axioms for arousing pity and fear, no doubt followed more thoughtful deliberation, and carries more significance. "Rebellion is an important process in the development of any art form," Spencer allows, but he supplies a caveat: "First, you need to get some idea of what you're rebelling against." In effect, Spencer is serving both the Aristotelians (directly) and the Brechtians (indirectly) by offering an introduction to the fundamentals of Western drama, which nascent playwrights may then observe, disregard, or rebut as they see fit. Perhaps most significant, though, is how Spencer's book puts dramatists on guard against a truly insidious adversary, pseudo-rebellion, which reveals itself in a number of irritating mannerisms – zaniness, petulance, ear-splitting volume, or reckless, inexpert pacing – and accounts for the precarious, nearly invisible presence in our culture of a medium rejected as inauthentic.

In numerous ways, *The Playwright's Guidebook* is analogous to two posthumous works by fiction writer John Gardner, *On Becoming a Novelist* (1983) and *The Art of Fiction* (1984). Like the latter, Spencer's book originated as seminar notes that got reshaped over years of classroom instruction and finally found their way into print. And like Gardner, who was a university professor, a novelist, and editor of a literary journal, Spencer not only is a playwright who teaches playwriting (at Sarah Lawrence College) but also served as literary manager for the Ensemble Studio Theatre in New York, where he claims to have waded through two thousand submitted scripts a year. Both include in their texts writing exercises which I can't imagine any reader will bother to complete, and both indulge in obligatory hand wringing about whether or not writing can even be taught, before reaching the common-sense conclusion that, like painters, musicians, and dancers, writers can at least be assisted in answering their calling through informed and conscientious instruction.

Like Spencer, Gardner emphasized the importance of having the rules of writing down cold before attempting the subtle art of suspending the rules. And yet he contradicted himself, in a perfectly reasonable way, by declaring that in writing there are no rules. The search for aesthetic absolutes is a misapplication of the writer's energy, he claimed. "When one begins to be persuaded that certain things must never be done in fiction and certain other things must always be done, one has entered the first stage of aesthetic arthritis, the disease that ends up in pedantic rigidity and the atrophy of intuition." Spencer's tutelage is more strict. "The rules of drama are the rules of nature," he commands. Aristotle, in his *Poetics*, was a categorizer – almost a scientist – not an advocate, as Artaud surely was. Therefore, Aristotle's observations on theater are similar to those of Newton and Einstein, Spencer claims: "they did not make the laws of physics, they only revealed them."

What Aristotle revealed was the basic Three-Act structure of the dramatic dream, which a playwright may develop over five acts (as did Shakespeare, or Shakespeare's publisher), two acts (the current convention), four acts (see Chekhov), or a single scene. The action of the play is driven by the protagonist's need or desire for something, revealed in Act One; conflict is provided in Act Two when a rival character, circumstance, or force of nature prevents the protagonist from getting what he wants; and a decisive event in Act Three brings resolution to the conflict. It is the nature of the conflict's dénouement that determines if the protagonist's needs are fulfilled or go unmet – which, Spencer comments, serves as "a good working definition of comedy versus tragedy."

Almost immediately, Spencer tells us, the Aristotelian rules for drafting a play – which Spencer renames *tools* – meet with resistance when introduced to his playwriting students, who demand greater flexibility. "They're afraid the tools will drain their work of creativity and that if they employ them, it will be embarrassingly obvious to the audience, who will see the play's scaffolding." Spencer instructs his students not to fear the power of dramatic structure, which taps into our subconscious mind. He implores them instead to harness that power to their own advantage. "We don't bemoan the fact that water flows downhill," he notes. "We put in a hydroelectric power plant."

Yet Spencer obviously has misgivings himself, as evidenced by the insertion of the euphemistic *tools* as a distancing device against the inflexible term *rules*. Like John Gardner, he is ultimately tripped up by the incongruity inherent in every writer's manual. The author must insist that the rules of writing be catalogued and acknowledged – this is the book's *raison d'être* – while conceding that there are no rules in any absolute sense. "Many great plays do not use the tools I'm presenting here," Spencer concedes, "or if so, they use them in such idiosyncratic fashion that they are almost impossible to identify." This implies that the key to exploiting Aristotelian structure successfully may lie in part in disguising its use. The instinctive fear of Spencer's students, then – the fear of being too obvious – might serve them well in practice.

Even more rigidly than Spencer's book, the theater essays of David Mamet impose structural demands on drama which then necessitate feats of camouflage from the practicing writer. As noted in the previous essay, Mamet's definition of tragedy is more confining than Spencer's. For Mamet, a tragedy is not a play in which the Third-Act event is a harbinger of failure, leaving the protagonist unfulfilled; rather, it is a work in which the protagonist fully succeeds in getting what he desires (for example, knowledge of who has brought the plague upon Thebes), then realizes how misguided his desires were. What he wanted all along and successfully pursued brings not fulfillment but ruin. I can think of two recent examples from film in which these rigid strictures are adhered to with spectacular results: David Lynch's *Mulholland Drive*, in which Naomi Watts, ineffectually dissuaded by Greek chorus Laura Elena Harring, concludes her amateur sleuthing by climbing through the window of a locked apartment (which reeks of a decomposing body – her own); and Anthony Minghella's reworking of Patricia Highsmith's novel *The Talented Mr. Ripley*, where the threat of exposure necessitates that Ripley murder the only person who truly cares about him. By successfully transforming himself into a fake somebody (fulfillment of his desire), his fate is worse than if he had remained a true nobody (his original definition of failure).

But the lengths to which these screenwriters go to harness power from the same subconscious stream Sophocles tapped are extreme: they people their works with sociopaths, contravene the rules of time, even upend the very dream logic that justifies Aristotle's analysis in the first place. Unless one hits upon a brilliant ending, as Minghella did, or happens to be a narrative magician, like Lynch, one is well advised to relax or even disregard rules offered by an authority figure when their main effect is to box in the writer. But I believe Spencer has given us the Goldilocks formula here: the location of his rules along the rigidity/flexibility continuum feels just right. And he never permits fashion or its deadlier cousin, anti-fashion, to misdirect the course of his instruction.

It is worth noting, briefly, the fourth possible outcome of Aristotle's Three-Act structure: a decisive event that indicates failure on the part of the protagonist (say, death) but which ironically brings fulfillment (through redemption, resurrection, and eternal life). This is not to be confused with a *deus ex machina* ending, which interrupts the plot just before the dénouement, saving the protagonist from ruin. Rather, this scenario requires that the protagonist suffer, if temporarily. It resonates with the sunny platitudes of Christian instruction – "God doesn't close a door without opening a window" – and with the very core of Christian theology, but it had no place in the drama of ancient Greece and seems not to have secured a toehold in the Western theater tradition since the Renaissance. Ours is a tradition trapped in the individual psyche – a psyche that, in moments of unmediated self-awareness, dreads the finality of death.

Brecht's theories on theater – and his attempts at undermining Aristotelian structure – would seem to have nothing in common with this optimistic inversion of tragic irony. Brecht set out deliberately to alienate the audience from the emotional experience of drama, thereby lending clarity to the text's social and political relevance. In both types of narrative, though, the individual's innate dream processes are distorted out of a sincere sense of duty, to a benign creator in one instance, to mankind in the other. Whatever social, political, or religious obligations Spencer may feel he and fellow playwrights work under, these do not in his mind outweigh the aesthetic obligation imposed on every artist, requiring him to satisfy the needs of the human subconscious. "The most important single notion in the theory of fiction I have outlined," wrote John Gardner, "is that of the vivid and continuous fictional dream." Similarly, Spencer warns his playwriting students not to disregard this notion as applied to drama, at least not without good reason and – a trickier point – sufficient talent. "When idiosyncratic conventions are badly done," he observes, "the audience feels confused and let down, as though they're aware the playwright had something to say but lacked the means to say it." He allows for idiosyncrasies in artists he admires, like Robert Wilson, whose visions defy Aristotle's schema as well as the theories of Carl Jung and other twentieth-century psychologists. ("There is no action in his theater," Spencer notes about Wilson, "no conflict, no event.") But – a bit too conveniently – he recategorizes Wilson's work as *theater*, not drama, to avoid the messiness of self-contradiction.

Spencer does not, however, place other classic anti-Aristotelian works, like *Waiting for Godot*, outside the realm of drama proper. Yet Samuel Beckett's famous play lacks the third key element of traditional dramatic structure: a decisive event. The protagonists desire the arrival of Godot, they are blocked in achieving their desire by his delay, but there is no resolution to the conflict – just more indeterminate delay. "Only a person who deeply understands the theory of [...] the dramatic event could write a play like *Waiting for Godot*," Spencer plausibly tells his students. But the fact remains: the play does not answer what Spencer calls the Passover question – Why is this night different from all other nights? Or rather it does answer, but in a disheartening way: This night is no different.

After acknowledging that *Godot* succeeds on its own terms, Spencer releases his students to their own creative impulses, having exhorted them – possibly in vain – to exploit the wisdom of past practitioners and theorists. It is natural for writers to distance themselves from predecessors, as Harold Bloom made clear in *The Anxiety of Influence*. John Gardner remarked that only some of the earliest literature – parts of the Biblical and Homeric texts – are entirely free of the deconstructive impulse. "If the business of the first man is to create," he observed, "the business of the second is at least partly to correct." What Stuart Spencer prudently anticipates is the misalignment of a young writer's basic worldview and talent with the actual execution of his or her deconstructive art. One cannot teach integrity, one can only implore. The key literary ingredients happened to reverberate in the works of Beckett, an existentialist for whom every day was "unbearably very much like another," as Spencer puts it. But less gifted artists may find themselves constructing arbitrary, inorganic narratives, hoping to please the wrong people (academics, critics, artistic directors, other playwrights) at the cost of displeasing the people who count (themselves, audience members). This leads to pseudo-rebellious works. Peter Brook, whose book-length essay *The Empty Space* Spencer recommends to his students, wrote, "It is foolish to allow a revulsion from bourgeois forms to turn into a revulsion from needs that are common to all men." I would add that this revulsion is especially foolish when it is not innate but, rather, imposed from without.

Spencer cites an essay from *American Theatre* magazine in which the author vents her frustration over the pressures placed on her and others in the theater to "push the envelope" and eschew the conventions of narrative at all cost. This premium placed on the insubordinate and unconventional, at least in major regional markets, is confirmed by the current publicity campaign of a blue-chip theater in my hometown. Its season is advertised as "extreme" and "edgy" though the productions include A.R. Gurney's *Far East* and two plays by Kenneth Lonergan – all fine works, but not the cutting edge of the avant-garde. My local theater promotes these plays as *outré* out of some weird compulsion I can't explain, since I know of no regular theater patron who considers "edgy" and "extreme" to be positive rather than neutral attributes. A fractious, unorthodox play can be good or bad, compelling or dull, just like more conventional works. In fact, the odds of success are probably lower for a defiantly rebellious commodity, since the playwright has chosen the rougher road (Spencer: "in writing, there's nothing wrong with taking the easy way out") and because the play has been sold as the latest thing, assigning to it a limited shelf life that invites a newer "latest thing" to come along and knock it into the bargain bin of expired goods.

Potential audience members to whom the term *theater* suggests puerile imitations of famous works by rebel playwrights turn out faithfully for professional sports teams and second-tier rock 'n' roll acts from past generations but balk at the cost of a theater ticket and dismiss drama *in toto* as difficult, obscure, and pretentious. Thus the most immediate, red-blooded form of storytelling – live theater – is shunned as anti-social and remote. Even *Waiting for Godot* itself, which continues to prove useful to university instructors precisely because it clearly demonstrates anti-Aristotelian impulses at work, has limited relevance for audiences beyond the classroom. Camille Paglia has described attending a production of the play as a university undergraduate in the 1960s, when the newly energized popular culture of the United States – "rude, vital, brassy" – had already swept off the stage the emotionally repressed, "spinsterish" notions typified by a work so intellectualized and clever that it disregards the requisite elements of its own narrative genre. Beckett's place in theater history is assured, but the visceral impact of his work on audience members is equivocal.

A final irony of dramatic literature is that, in contrast to Tolstoy's dictum about families, it is the pugnacious, contrarian, "unhappy" plays which are too much the same, or at least seem so at the deepest and most automatic level of human cognition. Every play subsequent to *Waiting for Godot* that omits a decisive event from its Third Act is a pale imitation, adhering anachronistically to Beckett's specific political and intellectual concerns circa 1952, whereas every play subsequent to *Oedipus* that skillfully exploits the Three-Act structure revealed by Aristotle pleases in its own way – or seems to, which is all that matters. To assist playwrights in avoiding the trap of intellectualized banality and sameness, Spencer instructs them to value not the heart over the head, but the subconscious over the conscious. "The conscious mind will always try to take over the writing of your play, and will do so if you let it," Spencer warns. "It thinks that it always knows best." But it is wrong. "You have to put your conscious mind on hold long enough for the subconscious to do the work that only it can do." And that unfettered work will almost certainly draw the playwright back to narrative structures that have stood for millennia, and to the basic patterns of the human brain.

[2003]

Wither [sic] Theater?

Does American drama stand a chance at being resuscitated? Three rising stars – David Schulner, Craig Wright, and Melissa James Gibson – have new works available from Dramatists Play Service that offer an overview of where the genre might be heading, and the outlook appears grim.

Of the three, David Schulner seems most naturally attracted to interesting and sound ideas, and he apparently appreciates the business end of things as well: his single-set, two-character play, *An Infinite Ache*, should function as catnip for regional theaters, to use Richard Greenberg's phrase, owing to its main concern – a romantic relationship – and minimal cost demands. The play premiered on the second stages of the Long Wharf Theatre in New Haven, CT, and the Old Globe in San Diego. The age of the two characters (mid-to-late twenties) further raises the financially attractive possibility of nonequity casting.

After a first dinner date, Hope and Charles stop by his studio apartment and dance around the dual looming possibilities of sex and a second date. Much like Schulner himself, the characters are just embarking on their careers. "I'm a historian," Charles states when Hope asks him what he does. "No, but for money," she clarifies.

Not due to a magic spell or intervention from the gods, but simply by virtue of theatrical convention, the characters move speedily through time, acting out the entire arc of their nascent relationship. The plot moves ahead without expositional pauses, speed bumps, or segues. "Isn't it great to get past that lovey, touchy, constant sex phase of the relationship?" Hope asks a few minutes into the play.

> CHARLES (trying hard). Sure.
> HOPE. By now we should be making something, building something, right?
> CHARLES. Probably.
> HOPE. Since we've reached a plateau and we have to go to the next level.
> CHARLES. Kind of.
> HOPE. We're just coasting slowly down hill, aren't we?
> CHARLES. Not really.
> HOPE. Things are completely dead between us, aren't they?
> CHARLES. Not at all.
> HOPE. And I think we should stop seeing each other.
> CHARLES. When did this happen?
> HOPE. I've been trying to tell you.
>   (Hope exits.)

The abruptness of the action on stage exaggerates (only slightly) the fickle nature of most relationships. Hope and Charles reconcile, and what ensues resembles a fantasy marriage meant to ward off the frustrations of serial monogamy. Not that their union is idyllic: they suffer through tight money, the death of an infant, religious differences, couples therapy, a rebellious teenage daughter ("Let's move and not tell her"), empty-nest syndrome, infidelity, further reconciliation, second careers, the death of parents, and old age. Moreover, the "infinite ache" of the title refers not to a nagging, limitless emotional investment in love but, rather, to the sad inability of romantic attraction to hold its grip.

"I thought love was supposed to be stronger than this," the elderly Charles observes. But for all of the gloom surrounding the conventional parameters of these characters' lives, Schulner's theme is highly conservative: the institutions society attempts to impose on us in our youth – marriage, parenthood, career – are too valuable to forgo, he suggests, no matter how disappointing they may ultimately prove to be. The play's prospective account of the couple's relationship underscores an essential truth: the decision to settle down and build a family is not inevitable, but it is often desirable.

Schulner makes a few bad minor decisions, like having Charles, newly arrived in Los Angeles, tell Hope she is the first woman he's met there who doesn't want to be an actress, and making Charles awkwardly raise the nonissue of Hope's family background (part Chinese, part Filipina). These struck me as television moments and, indeed, the author was a staff writer for the series *Once and Again*. But the playwright's command of dialogue is generally excellent. Even more impressive, Schulner manages somehow to make the play's inevitable return from the speculative future to the concrete present not seem like a letdown or a cop-out.

In short, Schulner is hugely gifted, and surprisingly intelligent for a playwright (forgive me, but it's true). His other works, including the biblical adaptation *Isaac* and *This Thing of Darkness*, a collaboration with Craig Lucas, are not yet published, nor have they been staged in Washington, DC, where I live, but I am eager to see and read them both. Schulner, still in his late twenties, has been commissioned to write new plays for South Coast Repertory, Actors' Theatre of Louisville, and the Joseph Papp Public Theater, among many others. His is a playwriting career about to explode.

Craig Wright's career is also ascendant, but his I.Q. seems to be closer to the national playwright average. *The Pavilion* and a newer, as yet unpublished work, *Recent Tragic Events*, reveal an author unable to mesh theme with character and plot. Making matters worse, the themes he chooses – predestination versus free will, the unidirectional nature of time – are banal when addressed explicitly, and he attacks them with the eager innocence of a student in freshman writing class.

The Pavilion requires a cast of three – a man and a woman, both age thirty-seven, plus a narrator – and its setting is suggested by a pair of benches. Like *An Infinite Ache*, this is a work that frees up funds and allows a regional theater to stage more elaborate productions in the same season.

"This is the way the universe begins," the narrator opens the play. "A raindrop (that isn't really a raindrop) drops, like a word, 'rain' *drops*, into a pool (that isn't really a pool, more like a pool of listening minds)."

Might I instead suggest simply, "A raindrop falls into a pool of listening minds." The passage would thereby gain something by way of clarity. But if, stripped of the author's backpedaling and self-contradiction, the narrator's sentiments then appear nonsensical – the universe, after all, does not begin when a raindrop falls into a pool of listening minds – then perhaps one shouldn't use that bogus imagery at all.

The narrator assumes the voice of numerous characters attending a twenty-year high school class reunion, standing in for classmates of the two leads, Peter, a psychologist relocated to Minneapolis, and Kari, a bank employee who remained in their small Minnesota town. The narrator also makes further cosmic pronouncements: "In human history, every little thing makes a difference." (Patently false.) "At the center of everything in the universe, there's you." (True in its way, but not something anyone needs to hear – and a sentiment that facilitates Peter's irritating solipsism.) Kari issues similar statements. "Because of you, the entire universe is ruined ... forever!" she screams at Peter, who abandoned her, pregnant and alone, after graduation.

"This is a play about time," Peter informs us in the second act. This bit of information has value: the narrator's ominous ruminations notwithstanding, it wasn't clear heading into intermission what the author was getting at. Was he interested in forgiveness? Or the reshaping of personalities? Was the narrative, like *An Infinite Ache*, a meditation on the inevitable waning intensity of relationships, especially marriage? Or was it about infidelity, and one's right to urge others to pursue infidelity as well? Peter claims to regret that he "got on the wrong train" twenty years earlier – "I wish I had fought harder to do what was right" – yet his efforts to remedy the situation suggest he is an unsavory character who believes he deserves to have it all, not a contrite soul wishing to atone for past mistakes.

After asking Kari's husband for permission to have a heart-to-heart talk with his wife, so that they might put their painful history behind them, Peter – no wiser or more ethically centered than at age seventeen – encourages Kari to abandon her marriage and run away with him to the Twin Cities. "You're such a weirdo!" Kari shouts, and indeed at times it seemed possible that the playwright intended Peter to be clinically demented. But much else in the play resists this interpretation. We are clearly meant to sympathize with Peter and curse the limitations the universe has placed on his happiness. Wright lacks both the insight to make his philosophical observations compelling and the theater savvy to make Peter's plight sympathetic, or his motivations consistent. The writing here is careless to the point of irresponsibility. And – I can't stress this enough – the characters' central conflict has nothing legitimately to do with the cosmic forces of the universe that the narrator prattles on about.

In a subsequent work, *Recent Tragic Events*, which premiered in August 2002 at Washington's Woolly Mammoth Theatre, Wright sets the action of the play on the evening of September 12, 2001, forcing the theme of free will versus predestination to (he believes) illuminate the attacks on New York City and Washington. He redeems himself somewhat by assigning his philosophical disquisitions to a liquored-up Joyce Carol Oates, portrayed by a sock puppet held by an actress wearing a Santana t-shirt and nothing below. In stark contrast to the irritating and incongruous theatrical gestures one usually encounters in plays attempting to "push the envelope," this is truly inspired. And yet, the playwright seems to have no idea that his very familiar observations – coulda, woulda, shoulda – are, if not offensive, then inappropriate and unwelcome in this context. The relatives of the September 11 victims no doubt replay that day in their minds, wishing somehow to save their loved ones through retroactive intervention, but in a literary work such an approach manages to waste every valid thematic possibility inherent in the material. Worse, Wright injects absurd coincidence into the equation: the lead male character realizes that he met his blind date's identical twin sister, by chance, weeks earlier, halfway across the country, and set her on a course toward her own demise in one of the towers. Is this a Brazilian soap opera? What was Wright thinking?

Wright's work left me more dispirited than did Melissa James Gibson's play *[sic]*, though Gibson's writing by design should have proven more irritating and disheartening. In *[sic]*, Gibson populates one floor of a New York City apartment building with three not-yet-middle-aged characters (composer Theo, editor Babette, and aspiring auctioneer Frank), places conventional conflicts in their path (petty jealousies, eviction, a corpse), then aborts her project. That is, she deliberately leaves it in an unsatisfying, nearly embryonic state, refusing to carry through on the plot ideas she started, or shape the dialogue into speakable form.

The fact that Babette works as an editor – of an "Outbursts Text" – is, I believe, key to understanding the playwright's designs. The dialogue in the play is arch and redundant and comes in a torrent of words with inconsistent punctuation and arbitrary line breaks, as if a word processor were spitting out the playwright's rough draft.

> BABETTE: I'm going to the store downstairs Do you need anything from
>   The Store Downstairs
> THEO: No Uh Yes I need candy bars Could you pick me up some
>   Candy Bars
> BABETTE: How many candy bars
> THEO: Six or seven Candy Bars
> BABETTE: Six
>   Or Seven candy bars
> THEO: Seven Candy Bars

I am willing to concede that the singular and extreme displeasure I derive from such passages may be peculiar to me and shared by no one else – I hope it is – but this much is objectively true: huge chunks of Gibson's dialogue fill up space but do not serve the plot. This applies especially to long, irrelevant conversations we overhear, conducted by others in the building, and excerpts from the cassette tape Frank listens to as part of his auctioneer training. Whatever Gibson may be telling us about the inadequacies of language and modern communication, her methods are repellent, which may be her intention (thus, the title *[sic]*). She has chosen to stage and publish what appears to be a raw, unedited version of a play manuscript, with digressions, multiple phrasings, and messy, spontaneous insertions all allowed to stand. This is an unwise idea of the sort Stephen Sondheim might have built an entire musical around.

[2003]

Afterword: A Not So Safe Space

The following press release was issued on September 17, 2001:

> We at Golden Thread Productions wish to offer our deepest sympathy and heartfelt condolences to all who have lost a loved one at the September 11, 2001 tragedy, and join the world community in condemning these inhumane and atrocious acts. Since its inception, Golden Thread Productions has been dedicated to exploring the Middle Eastern culture and identity in all its complexity. Therefore, we feel as a company that now more than ever it is crucial to go forward with a cultural event that we hope will foster a deeper understanding of our shared humanity and shatter the commonly held stereotypes associated with the Middle East.

The cultural event in question was ReOrient 2001, a festival of short plays scheduled to include my one-act *Expatriates*. Prior to receiving the press release, I failed to consider what impact the hijackings might have on the Bay Area theater group, a majority of whose members are Middle Eastern immigrants. Numbed by a sense of impending personal doom (I live in Washington, D.C., six blocks from the White House), I thought only of myself and the coincidental timing: *Expatriates* has as its backdrop the obtuseness and complacency of Westerners threatened by truck bombings in an unnamed Persian Gulf state. It was accepted for inclusion in the festival four months prior to the September 11 attacks. I would now be credited with a prescience of an unwelcome sort.

Previously undecided about attending the festival, I felt a sudden obligation to attend and a sense of privilege at being included. There were selfish motives as well. Like academia, the theater establishment boasts of its eagerness to challenge reigning orthodoxies while actually protecting them. Over the previous two years, in fact, I'd written a collection of essays on this very theme – that self-proclaimed theater rebels rarely broach contentious subjects. But in San Francisco, I would finally have a chance to contest some of the intelligentsia's most cherished assumptions (Western culture is egregiously intolerant, pacifism guarantees our security), if not through my stage work, which in this case was topical but not blatantly objectionable, then during after-performance Q&A sessions with the playwrights and other festival participants.

Upon arrival in California, I learned that three actors slated to perform in the festival backed out soon after September 11, fearing for their safety. With last-minute doubling of parts, the festival went on as scheduled. The director and cast made what I felt were some unfortunate performance choices: the only Arab character in *Expatriates* was played as a greasy Casanova (by an Arab actor, no less), and discussion of terrorist threats among the diplomat characters was conducted in solemn, hush-hush tones. (The point of the play is that safety considerations are strangely incidental to these Western hedonists, who are more concerned about playing tennis, securing forbidden pork and alcohol, and – at all times and in all places – career advancement.) But my general reaction to the production was one of delight.

Cast members, however, were less sanguine. In particular, a young actor of Palestinian descent was incensed that a Palestinian-American author opened each evening's performance by reading passages from her memoir-in-progress and answering a few questions immediately after. This delayed our curtain time and seemed to test the patience of audience members sitting in the sweltering theater; worse, the contents of the woman's book and her impromptu responses agitated the actor, who then found it impossible to get into character for his performance.

His main objection was that the memoirist, who had emigrated from Ramallah to San Francisco in the 1950s, was badly out of touch with contemporary Palestinian culture and politics and had no business making insider pronouncements about the present Israeli-Palestinian deadlock. I had my own reservations about linking her memoir to my work through simple proximity. By scheduling both the woman's reading and my play before intermission the artistic director had – deliberately or inadvertently – implied a connection between Israeli oppression of the Palestinians on one hand, and Wahhabi terrorism on the other. That seemed to me misleading.

Living in Riyadh in the mid-1990s, I witnessed the egregiously intolerant, antipluralistic impulses of Saudi culture that had given rise to the ongoing campaign to purify the Arabian peninsula of nonbelievers. Driving from Riyadh to Jidda, I encountered – at the Mecca city limits – the infamous traffic signs directing infidels around the periphery of the holy city, lest we defile it by our presence and suffer the prescribed punishment (death, of course). These devout bedouins, by submitting to God's will, had condemned themselves to a life of subordination, whereas Westerners, by challenging God's will through science and modern medicine, had reaped wealth, power, and long lives of pleasure and amusement. This confused and agitated the average Saudi, who had been promised great things in exchange for his piety by a God who either (1) was playing a sick joke, or (2) did not exist. Moreover, the Saudis, like most Arabs outside the Levant, are in general resentful if not hateful toward the Palestinians themselves, whom they see as ineffectual and weak-willed by comparison to the Israelis, and whose community in the Gulf states comprises mostly educated managerial types who hold the Saudis in contempt and resemble Westerners to an uncomfortable degree.

For these reasons I felt uneasy about the pairing of my play with a consideration of the Palestinian problem, but as I sat in the audience listening to the woman read from her memoir, I found the excerpts compelling. She had an open, ebullient personality and a strong speaking voice, which counts for a lot on stage. And as a former State Department employee, I recognized the truth in her accusation that American foreign policy toward Israel is not *dictated*, as so many Arabs insist, but strongly influenced by a powerful domestic lobby with only one counterpart of comparable strength: the immigrant community in Miami that has shaped America's similarly disastrous, unnuanced policy toward Cuba over the past four decades.

Because the Palestinian-American author held a brief Q&A session of her own, she did not participate in the company's post-performance talks, which remained exceptionally polite in tone, even tepid. Several attendees praised the theater company for providing a "safe space" to discuss controversial issues: ethnic strife, Western intolerance, the Islamic threat. Even so, I lost my nerve. That is, I limited myself to noting parallels between passages of dialogue from my play, written three years earlier, and questions we were now asking ourselves about the risks of commercial air travel or opening envelopes. I deliberately avoided inflammatory topics, such as the Saudi tendency – echoed at present throughout the Arab world – to concoct a Jewish conspiracy on which to deflect blame for atrocities committed by Muslims. I may have been thrown by the "safe space" designation, which in academia – my regular milieu – suggests a forum in which one is free to support the reigning consensus with no threat of dissent or intellectual challenge. In such an environment, I hold my tongue.

On my third evening in San Francisco, I sat out the opening reading. We had a nearly full house, which made the theater stifling, and I had heard the author read the two previous nights. (She slipped out of the theater herself prior to the dramatic performances every evening; therefore, she couldn't have been slighted by my absence.) I found one of the actors, an Iranian immigrant, smoking a cigarette outside. We chatted about the warm October weather, and I asked about Tehran, which he said he'd visited a couple of times in the past decade.

"It's ugly," he reported. He meant that Iranians – like Arabs – give little attention to a home's façade. The interior, enjoyed by family and friends, was all that mattered. A bigger problem, he said, was the general tendency to build shabbily, forgo maintenance, demolish entire city blocks, and build shabbily again. It suggested to him a culture in decline, or one without solid bearings. "Still, the revolution has done some good," he began to explain, but he quickly got sidetracked. "We mustn't expect too much, though. This is the problem with the West. We think we can change a culture in one generation. You know, the Enlightenment did not reach the Middle East. So, modernization couldn't take hold that easily – that was the Shah's mistake, among many mistakes." He snubbed out his cigarette and seemed to arrive at his main point. "The Iranians, to this day, have no use for opposing points of view," he admitted. "I don't know when they ever will." He sighed. It was clearly a dilemma for him, having passed from one culture to another in young adulthood. "I guess I really don't know what I think. About the Middle East – I just don't know."

Inside, I took the last empty seat and watched my play for the third time. Following intermission the company staged the artistic director's own contribution to the festival, an absorbing autobiographical work that diagrams a daisy chain of intolerance and recrimination among several generations of Muslims, Armenian Christians, and Jews in Turkey and Palestine. Unknown to me, the Palestinian memoirist had not taken questions this evening after her reading. Agitated cast members had apparently prevailed upon the artistic director to cut short the woman's presentation. In exchange, she would return at the end of the evening for the general post-performance discussion. Or, more accurately, she would dominate it.

Her main theme for the session, it soon became clear, was her disgust at the depiction of Middle Easterners, especially Arabs, in the American media. Other panelists spoke of harassment they suffered upon arrival in the United States during the Iranian hostage crisis in the late 1970s. Their testimony echoed similar reports of violence and threats of violence following September 11. The Palestinian memoirist was intent on blaming the entire image problem, and ensuing "reprisal" attacks, on American journalists. For all their faults, though, the media seemed to me to have devoted a great deal of energy to exposing and condemning scattered incidents of ethnically motivated violence. For useful perspective, I was interested in comparing the American media's treatment of Middle Easterners with the treatment of Americans and Israelis in the Middle Eastern press. The Saudi media, for example, were tightly controlled by the monarchy; censorship of imported newspapers and magazines was stringent and, at times, quite silly. During my posting in Riyadh, an entire page of the *International Herald Tribune* was inked over by the censor's black magic marker before delivery to subscribers. Curious, I e-mailed friends in Europe. Was the offending item a book review of a controversial political volume? I inquired. A lingerie advertisement? A pro-Israeli feature? No, friends informed me. It was a recipe for pork chops.

But I chose not to challenge the tenor of the discussion, or change its direction. Not only was I certain my observations would be unwelcome in this forum, I was also intimidated by the memoirist's manner of speech: brash, resonant, loud. In contrast, I am cursed with a weak vocal instrument; in any confrontation, she would bellow over me. Plus, our age and gender differences interfered: the author reminded me of my mother.

A woman in the audience raised her hand. She addressed me by name. "I'd like to hear what your reaction was to Saudi Arabia," she said. And just like that, I was forced to make a decision: keep quiet, or talk. I'd twice heard the Palestinian author read from her memoir that members of a church she'd attended upon arrival in the United States neglected to invite her to Sunday dinner. This seemed a mild rebuke compared to my experience in Saudi Arabia, where churches are illegal and Filipino guest workers were routinely arrested and flogged for holding clandestine prayer services. I'd twice heard the author state she was a third-generation Quaker from Palestine – "How's that for demolishing stereotypes?" she asked; coincidentally, "Quaker" was the euphemism of choice for Jewish Americans who applied for work visas to Saudi Arabia, which required that applicants acknowledge their religion. (Openly Jewish applicants were summarily rejected.) I might have kept quiet, but it seemed just now the stakes were too high: our country was under attack, and my survival instincts surfaced. I was not about to permit a one-sided discussion to continue, having been handed this opening.

"To a Westerner, Saudi culture is very strange," I replied. "First-hand knowledge of it helps me understand the murderous impulses of the Wahhabi Muslims who are now intent on destroying the United States. In short, Saudi Arabia seems to me among the most intolerant cultures one could devise. If we wish to understand the current campaign of Arabist terror, we must look not to Jerusalem but to Jidda, Riyadh, and Mecca." I then turned to my fellow panelists. "When we criticize the failures of our own media or our culture in general, we hold ourselves to a very high standard – a standard of perfection, really. And I hope we always will. But relative to most Middle Eastern or Muslim cultures, ours is pluralistic and receptive to outsiders. Our media are a mixed bag, not a useless, monolithic institution as in the Middle East. If our self-critique is to have any value," I concluded, "we must acknowledge this as well."

Other panelists nodded their assent, but I saw the Palestinian-American author begin to shake violently. She screamed, "That's very hurtful to me!" And with the audience stunned into silence, she proceeded to lecture me at length.

Because the American media already distort the image of Arabs, she said, it is incumbent on the rest of us to say nothing negative about Arab cultures (even when unflattering observations are accurate). Besides, she continued screaming, the Saudis were until very recently isolated and provincial bedouins; we can't hold them to the same standards we hold other nationalities. I silently rejected the second argument out of hand, since I refuse to infantilize the Saudis, or any nationality for that matter. And her first point merely reiterated for me what is so fundamentally wrong with intellectual discourse today: especially in a university setting, in the humanities, one is obligated to disregard evidence that refutes an anti-Western thesis, rather than revise the thesis or abandon it altogether. Since September 11, I'd watched colleagues who had spent the past twenty years vilifying America for its puritanism and intolerance now mentally unable to categorize an assault by foreigners who object to our *permissiveness* and our secular notion of freedom, which they fear might spread.

Once the woman stopped shouting, I said, "I hadn't intended to be hurtful. I meant merely to add another piece to the puzzle."

She seemed not to hear me. The theater's artistic director interceded, directing the discussion to a different topic. I said nothing the rest of the evening.

Afterward, audience members expressed their opinion, privately, that I had been unfairly treated. And the Iranian-American actor I'd spoken to earlier made a point of shaking my hand. The next day, fellow panelists pulled me aside and expressed their concern that I not take offense. But I was not personally affronted by the outburst, coming from someone with much emotionally at stake in the topic. Nor did it alarm me that discussion of an important political issue had been thwarted, since the Palestinian woman's attempt to silence opposing views told the audience more about Middle Eastern culture than could any testimony I might have provided. What upset me was the symbolism of the act, in what had been declared a safe theatrical space. Given a chance to challenge the political orthodoxy on stage, I was, as usual, quickly told to shut up.

[2003]

Books Available from Gival Press

A Change of Heart by David Garrett Izzo
  1st edition, ISBN 1-928589-18-9, $20.00

  A historical novel about Aldous Huxley and his circle "astonishingly alive and accurate."
  — Roger Lathbury, George Mason University

Barnyard Buddies I by Pamela Brown; illustrations by Annie H. Hutchins
  1st edition, ISBN 1-928589-15-4, $16.00

  Thirteen stories filled with a cast of creative creatures both engaging and educational. "These stories in this series are delightful. They are wise little fables, and I found them fabulous."
  — Robert Morgan, author of *This Rock* and *Gap Creek*

Barnyard Buddies II by Pamela Brown; illustrations by Annie H. Hutchins
  1st edition, ISBN 1-928589-21-9, $16.00

  "Children's literature which emphasizes good character development is a welcome addition to educators' as well as parents' resources."
  — Susan McCravy, elementary school teacher

Bones Washed With Wine: Flint Shards from Sussex and Bliss by Jeff Mann
  1st edition, ISBN 1-928589-14-6, $15.00

  A special collection of lyric intensity, including the 1999 Gival Press Poetry Award winning collection. Jeff Mann is "a poet to treasure both for the wealth of his language and the generosity of his spirit."
  — Edward Falco, author of *Acid*

Canciones para sola cuerda / Songs for a Single String by Jesús Gardea;
  English translation by Robert L. Giron
  1st edition, ISBN 1-928589-09-X, $15.00

  A moving collection of love poems, with echoes of *Neruda à la Mexicana* as Gardea writes about the primeval quest for the perfect woman. "The free verse...evokes the quality and forms of cante hondo, emphasizing the emotional interplay of human voice and guitar."
  — Elizabeth Huergo, Montgomery College

Dead Time / Tiempo muerto by Carlos Rubio
  1st edition, ISBN 1-928589-17-0, $21.00

  This bilingual (English/Spanish) novel is "an unusual tale of love, hate, passion and revenge."
  — Karen Sealy, author of *The Eighth House*

Dervish by Gerard Wozek
  1st edition, ISBN 1-928589-11-1, $15.00

  Winner of the 2000 Gival Press Poetry Award. This rich whirl of the dervish traverses a grand expanse from bars to crazy dreams to fruition of desire. "By Jove, these poems shimmer."
  — Gerry Gomez Pearlberg, author of *Mr. Bluebird*

Dreams and Other Ailments / Sueños y otros achaques by Teresa Bevin
1st edition, ISBN 1-928589-13-8, $21.00

Winner of the Bronze Award – 2001 *ForeWord Magazine*'s Book of the Year Award for Translation. A wonderful array of short stories about the fantasy of life and tragedy but filled with humor and hope. "*Dreams and Other Ailments* will lift your spirits."
— Lynne Greeley, The University of Vermont

The Gay Herman Melville Reader by Ken Schellenberg
1st edition, ISBN 1-928589-19-7, $16.00

A superb selection of Melville's work. "Here in one anthology are the selections from which a serious argument can be made by both readers and scholars that a subtext exists that can be seen as homoerotic."
— David Garrett Izzo, author of *Christopher Isherwood: His Era, His Gang, and the Legacy of the Truly Strong Man*

Let Orpheus Take Your Hand by George Klawitter
1st edition, ISBN 1-928589-16-2, $15.00

Winner of the 2001 Gival Press Poetry Award. A thought provoking work that mixes the spiritual with stealthy desire, with Orpheus leading us out of the pit. "These poems present deliciously sly metaphors of the erotic life that keep one reading on, and chuckling with pleasure."
— Edward Field, author of *Stand Up, Friend, With Me*

Literatures of the African Diaspora by Yemi D. Ogunyemi
1st edition, ISBN 1-928589-22-7, $20.00

An important study of the influences in literatures of the world. "It, indeed, proves that African literatures are, without mincing words, a fountainhead of literary divergence."
—Joshua 'Kunle Awosan, University of Massachusetts Dartmouth.

Metamorphosis of the Serpent God by Robert L. Giron
1st edition, ISBN 1-928589-07-3, $12.00

"Robert Giron's biographical poetry embraces the past and the present, ethnic and sexual identity, themes both mythical and personal."
— *The Midwest Book Review*

Middlebrow Annoyances: American Drama in the 21st Century by Myles Weber
1st edition, ISBN 1-928589-20-0, $20.00

"Weber's intelligence and integrity are unsurpassed by anyone writing about the American theatre today...."
— John W. Crowley, The University of Alabama at Tuscaloosa

The Nature Sonnets by Jill Williams
1st edition, ISBN 1-928589-10-3, $8.95

An innovative collection of sonnets that speaks to the cycle of nature and life, crafted with wit and clarity. "Refreshing and pleasing."
— Miles David Moore, author of *The Bears of Paris*

Prosody in England and Elsewhere: A Comparative Approach by Leonardo Malcovati
1st edition, ISBN 1-928589-26-X, $16.00

"To write about the structure of poetry for a non-specialist audience takes a brave author. To do so in a way that is readable, in fact enjoyable, without sacrificing scholarly standards takes an accomplished author."
—Frank Anshen, State University of New York

The Smoke Week: Sept. 11-21, 2001 by Ellis Avery
1st edition, ISBN 1-928589-24-3, $15.00

Winner of the Ohioana Library Walter Rumsey Marvin Award
"Here is Witness. Here is Testimony."
— Maxine Hong Kingston, author of *The Fifth Book of Peace*

Songs for the Spirit by Robert L. Giron
1st edition, ISBN 1-928589-08-1, $16.95

This humanist psalter reflects a vision of the new millennium, one that speaks to readers regardless of their spiritual inclination. "This is an extraordinary book."
— John Shelby Spong, author of *Why Christianity Must Change or Die: A Bishop Speaks to Believers in Exile*

Tickets to a Closing Play by Janet I. Buck
1st edition, ISBN 1-928589-25-1, $15.00

Winner of the 2002 Gival Press Poetry Award
"...this rich and vibrant collection of poetry [is] not only serious and insightful, but a sheer delight to read."
— Jane Butkin Roth, editor, *We Used to Be Wives: Divorce Unveiled Through Poetry*

Wrestling with Wood by Robert L. Giron
3rd edition, ISBN 1-928589-05-7, $5.95

A chapbook of impressionist moods and feelings of a long-term relationship which ended in a tragic death. "Nuggets of truth and beauty sprout within our souls."
— Teresa Bevin, author of *Havana Split*

For Book Orders Only, Call: 800.247.6553
Or Write : Gival Press, LLC / PO Box 3812 / Arlington, VA 22203
Visit: www.givalpress.com

www.ingramcontent.com/pod-product-compliance
Lightning Source LLC
Chambersburg PA
CBHW031633160426
43196CB00006B/393